FIRST ELEVENS

FIRST ELEVENS

The birth of international football and the men who made it happen

Andy Mitchell

best wishes

Andy Mitchell

First Elevens: the birth of international football

First published 2012 by Andy Mitchell Media, Scotland.
Contact: andymitchellmedia@gmail.com

ISBN: 978-1475206845

The author
Andy Mitchell sat on the Scotland bench at the opening match of the 1998 World Cup, but sadly was not called upon to face Brazil. As head of communications at the Scottish FA, he saw international football up close when he travelled with the Scotland team from the Faroes to the Far East, and now works as a media officer for UEFA. Passionate about sports history, he is on the selection panel for the Scottish Sports Hall of Fame and is a member of the British Society of Sports History.

Previous publications
A short history of St Bernard's FC (1995)
The Scotland International Programme Guide (2008)
Arthur Kinnaird: First Lord of Football (2011)

Cover illustration based on William Ralston's drawings of the first association football international, published in *The Graphic*, 14 December 1872.
Cover designed by Maureen Mitchell Design, www.maureenmitchelldesign.com

Back cover image: detail from JJ Thomson's Scotland cap, which marked his appearance in the 1872 international (*courtesy of Scottish Football Museum*).

CONTENTS

INTRODUCTION

"Gentlemen desirous of representing England..."

WHAT IS it that brings countries to a standstill when their top players meet on the football field? Why play international football at all?

Ask those questions today, and fans will explain they share a reflected pride in their nation's sporting success, and lap up the passion of major tournaments. Players, for all their huge pay packets, still enjoy immense prestige in being asked to represent their country and most do so for no financial reward. Academics have answers, too: one bluntly suggests that nations attain their fullest expression in two ways – war and sport.

To fully understand the rationale of international football you have to go back to a spring day in 1870, when two teams of gentlemen amateurs representing England and Scotland faced up to each other on a cricket ground in London. Anglo-Scottish rivalry may have been less prevalent in the mid-Victorian era than at other periods in history, yet this encounter was fiercely contested on the pitch and cheered vociferously from the sidelines. Pride, passion, prestige – they have been there from the start.

The global phenomenon of international football has its roots with those doughty pioneers. Although it takes a leap of imagination to link that event, watched by 'an assemblage of spectators such as is rarely seen' (about five hundred), with the hundreds of millions who tune in to a World Cup final, the nationalistic fervour is unmistakeable.

This book begins with a detailed study of the events and context that led to the playing of the first football internationals under both association and rugby rules. There was a bitter struggle between the codes to be recognised as the 'true' footballing representatives of England and Scotland but in the end, both codes won: the international dimension was the making of each of them.

The early England v Scotland encounters in London are often referred to as 'pseudo-internationals' but I consider a more accurate description is that of unofficial internationals. Certainly, from the perspective of the players, there can be little doubt they considered themselves to be representing their countries, and the selectors made every effort to put out the best possible teams from suitably qualified players. Regardless of status, these football games were an attractive proposition because of the personalities who took part.

The Scotland v England game in November 1872 is generally considered the first official association football contest, but it could be argued that it was essentially between the FA and Queen's Park FC as the Scottish FA was not formed until March 1873. The same consideration applies to the first two rugby internationals, which were played before the foundation of the Scottish Rugby Union.

The second major part of this book comprises a biography of all the players who took part. While a few, such as Alcock, Clegg and Kinnaird remain well known, even today, there are numerous others whose moment of glory was fleeting. As anyone who has undertaken this kind of research will appreciate, it is no simple matter to identify with certainty someone whose name and initials appear in a Victorian newspaper. There are dead ends, mistakes in published sources, tedious hours spent trawling through archives; and there are also moments of joy as a long-lost relative answers a query and supplies a photo, or the discovery of a passing comment in a newspaper article that confirms an important detail. To find the players, my research led around the world, with connections to notable events ranging from the second Afghan War to the construction of the Australian transcontinental railway. Closer to home, I have tracked down descendants of players, visited gravestones, spent money on birth certificates and badgered local historical societies.

The outcome is, quite simply, fascinating: the people who brought international football to life ranged from decorated soldiers, senior politicians and country vicars to bankrupts, wife-beaters and even a convicted killer. Many were successful in sport and careers, then disappeared into the ether; they emigrated and made new lives, changed their names, acquired titles or honours, and an alarming number of them died young. Some of their stories have never been told before: who would guess, for example, that a Scotland international would be elected to serve three terms in the Wyoming legislature?

While some minor details remain unknown, it is now possible to paint an accurate picture of the early footballers of both the handling and the kicking codes. All those who played in the five unofficial internationals, the first Scotland v England association football encounter, and the inaugural rugby match, have been positively identified, many for the first time.

2

Although rugby and association football have changed out of recognition, one major issue faced in 1870 still resonates today, that of the criteria for international selection. The qualification of some men to play for the unofficial Scotland team, in particular, was hard to fathom: with insufficient players in London of Scottish birth, the selectors opted for men with an appropriate heritage; and if those selected failed to turn up for a match, there was no option but to turn to emergency substitutes, whose Scottishness was secondary to whether they had brought their boots.

This led, inevitably, to accusations that some Scots were imposters, with no entitlement to represent the country: a debate that is still alive today thanks to third generation Scots, brought up in England or elsewhere, playing for a motherland they only know from their granny's knee. The English were not immune, either, choosing players born in India and Ireland, and once the official series got underway, four 'unofficial' Scots internationalists – Morten, AK Smith, Chappell and Lindsay – were persuaded to don an England shirt with varying degrees of entitlement. (It is an issue, it should be added, which is not exclusive to these shores, with naturalised Brazilians turning out for Poland or Croatia, talented immigrants choosing France or Germany, and many similar cases.)

The birth of international football was at times chaotic but, as I recall some highlights of my own life watching Scotland, it was utterly worthwhile.

Acknowledgements

Researching the lives of over a hundred Victorian sportsmen, few of whom left personal memoirs or eye-witness accounts, would not have been possible without the assistance of a large body of dedicated individuals.

First, I must thank the sports historians whose groundwork made this book possible. David Rice's tenacious detective powers unearthed details of Scotland players that had never previously seen the light of day, and I doubt I would have been able to complete the profiles of the 1872 team without his help. The collective biographies of early footballers by Keith Warsop and John Blythe-Smart are indispensable reference points for research, to which can be added Rob Cavallini's history of Wanderers FC and Keith Booth's life of CW Alcock.

I am particularly pleased to have involved a number of direct descendants of the pioneers in this research, many of whom were previously unaware of great-grandfather's sporting prowess. While most were delighted at the discovery, it was not pleasant to be told, in one case, that you were descended from a murderous thug. In the course of my research, I have accumulated a large amount of genealogical detail and background information about the players and their families which I would, in principle, be happy to share with descendants and fellow researchers.

I thank the following for providing information, photos and encouragement: Malcolm Bailey (Charterhouse), Liz Eshmade (Genealogical Society of South Africa), Nor Hanisah binti Ahmad (Muzium Perak), Penny Hatfield (Eton College), Helen Hoy (Canterbury Museum), Tracy Loch (Township of Wilmot), Max Lombardi (Graceland Cemetery, Chicago), Richard McBrearty (Scottish Football Museum), Lindsay Robertson (Moray Burial Ground Research Group), Catherine Smith (Charterhouse), Bill Bailey, Hon. Caroline Best, Ken Bogle, Rita Boswell, Willie Cross, Sheena Daykin, Sue Fenn, Colin Ferguson, Jeanette Findlay, Alistair Gordon, John Hutchinson, Charles Inglis, Peter Jefferson Smith, Graham Johnson, Sandy Johnson, Bill Kalkhoven, Ann Lardeur, David and Wendy Morten, Mandi Munro, James Pearson, Carol de Poy, Gary Ralston, Michael Riordan, Charles Sale, Bobbi Smith, Rita Wellstead, David Weston, Rick Zimmerman and everyone else who has supported this project, with apologies to any names I may have inadvertently omitted.

I have acknowledged the copyright holders of images used in this book and, to the best of my knowledge, the remaining images are out of copyright. Please let me know if this is not the case.

As in my last book, *First Lord of Football*, the biography of Arthur Kinnaird, I owe a debt to the growing army of anonymous archivists who have digitised millions of newspapers, books and genealogical records, making them accessible online for the benefit of researchers. Chief among these are staff at the National Library of Scotland, the British Library, Google News Archive and the National Library of Australia (Trove), and I have also used various local sites such as the Wyoming Newspaper Archive. Within the football history community, there are numerous contributors to online forums, notably scottishleague.net, who readily share their knowledge. The number of sources of information continues to grow at an exponential rate, and I am sure that football researchers in years to come will make many new

4

discoveries about the people and places featured in this book, particularly as the quality of optical character recognition improves.

However, a word of caution: a close examination of contemporary newspaper reports of football matches often reveals a conflict in their descriptions of play and even the names they attributed to the participants. To an extent, these discrepancies were understandable when there were late call-offs, but there was also a carelessness about some reports, with spellings and initials varying from paper to paper. I have made every effort to check facts and references, but sometimes this has simply not been possible, and if there are any errors they are entirely my own.

Finally, I offer warm thanks to my parents, Angus and Ann Mitchell, for their encouragement and assiduous proof-reading, and to my wife, Maureen, not only for the superb cover design but also for her continued and unflagging support.

Andy Mitchell
Bridge of Allan
May 2012

Chapter 1

A PERFECT PASSION

Who played football in 1870, and why

IT WAS almost dark. Caked in mud, John Cockerell could hardly tell who was on his own side. Not that it mattered much, there were no winners, no goals.

Bruised from heavy charges and aggressive tackling, the young London businessman limped off the pitch and nipped into the shed that served as a dressing room to change his outer clothes. Someone had a bucket of water which helped to wipe off the worst of his facial mask. It was a long trek in the gathering gloom from Battersea Park to his home in Camberwell, but he felt refreshed and ready to face the challenges of the working week ahead. Ah, football! Great game.

Players such as Cockerell subscribed to the adage expressed in the world's first book on football: 'The game has been with me a perfect passion.'[1] He'd be back next week for more, but didn't yet know where, or for which team.

Although the Football Association had come into being in 1863, its brand of kicking football was still finding its feet as it approached the end of the decade. Their laws of the game were still being chopped and changed, and opposing captains had to meet before each match and agree on the rules. Teams came and went, so did the players, matches were played on public parks, and it had not yet become a spectator sport. It was all a bit of a shambles.

There was strong rivalry from clubs playing rugby football rules, with their emphasis on handling, which was popular in London, Lancashire and Scotland. The FA did not even have a monopoly of football played with the feet, with established clubs in Sheffield, Nottingham and elsewhere playing to their own rules.

Other sports, on the other hand, were flourishing. Cricket was so well established that it could attract 20,000 to Lord's for Eton v Harrow, the Civil Service Sports mustered six thousand at Beaufort

House, and vast crowds banked the Thames for the Boat Race and other major rowing contests; out of town, hordes would flock to horse races and boxing contests.

At that point, no-one could have foreseen how association football would explode onto the public consciousness over the next ten years, establishing itself as the national game: in 1870, the first attempt at international football was made; 1871 saw the start of the FA Cup; in 1872 came the first official international, followed closely, in 1873, by the formation of a national association in Scotland. And so it continued on an exponential scale until, by 1880, there were thousands of clubs, five-figure crowds for major matches, and professional players (albeit paid under the table). Football went from amateur kick-about to professional business in the space of a decade.

To understand why this happened, and how internationals gave football a crucial new dimension, it is necessary to go a little further back. Before 1850, few sporting contests involved an appreciable amount of travel. There were occasional cricket and rowing matches between schools and the universities, individual boxers and pedestrians at the top of their game might be lured by prize money to venture forth, but generally sport was a local affair. That changed largely thanks to the growth of the railways, which provided accessible and affordable travel, and the growth of a middle class with time for leisure.

Football, which had become virtually extinct in its traditional country form, started to emerge as an urban sport in the late 1850s. However, the biggest stumbling block to inter-club matches was the lack of a common set of rules as it was pointless playing against another outfit if each side had a different understanding of fundamental principles. Matches were only feasible if the teams could agree on how it should be played, which was not often because the game had tended to grow up according to local conditions at schools, which varied from enclosed cloisters to wide open spaces. The need for a mutually acceptable set of rules was paramount if football was to expand.

Although consensus was reached in some cities, notably Sheffield and Edinburgh, in London the tipping point came in 1863 with the formation of the Football Association, but only after several weeks of argument provoked a split between those who wanted hacking and those who did not. The rugby football fraternity went their own way, much to the chagrin of those who considered that the ability to endure pain was the mark of a true sportsman.

The FA's clubs embarked on a slow and stuttering progress, dogged by constant discussions about the laws of the game. The offside rules, charging from behind, throw ins and use of the hands were particularly hot topics, and match reports are also peppered with differing methods of scoring such as rouges, touchdowns and bases, as well as goals. Some things don't change, however, and it was possible right from the start to score an own goal – a concept that was never taken up by rugby football.

What the best dressed footballers might wear: a loose shirt and white cotton duck trousers. This image was on the cover of Routledge's *Football*, published 1867

The season's fixture list comprised a mixture of matches not just between clubs, but also against public schools and university colleges which had the advantages of regular practice, dedicated playing space and somewhere to get changed. Otherwise, the clubs played wherever they could: the open spaces of Battersea Park or Clapham Common, the outfield of cricket pitches, even private estates. The boundaries of play were marked by flags, the goals were two posts stuck in the ground with a tape slung between them, and playing costumes were rudimentary: hard boots, long cotton duck[2] trousers, and a loose shirt. Many players wore caps or cowls, as much through social custom as to be able to identify the sides.

Matches would generally last an hour and a half, and, although Saturday was the preferred day for a match, those with the leisure to take time off during the week had plenty of opportunities for football. Eleven-a-side was the optimal number, in line with the games played at Eton, Harrow and Westminster, but it was a regular occurrence for teams to arrive without a full complement of players (or sometimes with too many players) and the number of participants could vary; it was not unusual to have, say, seven against eleven. Sometimes, efforts were made to even up the sides, using anyone handy or borrowing members of the opposition as an 'emergency'; at other times, the sides simply played with whatever resources they had: it seemed not to matter.

This frightening view of English football as a mass fight was published in 1868 by a French magazine, *Le Journal Illustré*.

There was almost a casual approach to club loyalty, and a player could be a member of several different clubs. The better ones would jump from club to club, depending on who asked them to turn out on any given weekend, and there was certainly nothing to stop a man playing for and against his 'own' club in successive weeks. Playing the game was considered more important than loyalty to the jersey.

Tactics were basic, and although passing was not unknown, usually the game was based on a player dribbling with the ball, backed up by his colleagues and faced by opponents who formed a defensive wall to block their path. It was often a trial of strength, with the ball trapped within heaving mass 'bullies' or scrimmages as each team strove to gain possession of the ball and kick it in the direction of goal. The emphasis was on attack, yet so effective was the mass defence that goal-scoring was at a premium. A match without goals was still regarded as a useful exercise, and football as a sport presented an opportunity to demonstrate controlled aggression, using bodily strength and teamwork to gain an advantage. Yet, for all the rough and tumble nature of the play, reports of fights or violence were almost unheard of. It was, after all, a game for gentlemen.

One of the earliest football team photos is this group of Charterhouse boys in 1863. It includes the Muir Mackenzie brothers, who would both play for Scotland in the unofficial internationals. Kenneth is third from left, Montague is far right.
(*reproduced by kind permission of the Headmaster and Governors of Charterhouse*)

A glance through the background of London's players in 1870 shows a clear bias towards the public schools, with the scions of Eton, Harrow, Charterhouse and Westminster dominating. Football clubs were mainly formed by their Old Boys who entered a career straight from school as well as those who went up to the universities of Cambridge and Oxford.

There were football sections within the Civil Service and the army (initially for the officers only), and other clubs were formed as

11

offshoots of rowing and cricket clubs. For those without a top public school background, for example those who had attended Brentwood Grammar School in Essex or Clapham Grammar in south London, there were 'open' clubs such as NNs (No Names) of Kilburn, Barnes and Clapham Rovers. These were particularly appropriate for players whose principal qualification was wealth, notably those with 'new money'. Their common bond was being sufficiently well-off to be able to afford leisure time to take part in sports and, so long as they behaved like gentlemen, they were welcome. This social demographic would soon change and, for example, the Scotland players of the first international, in November 1872, included the sons of bakers, clerks and gardeners, with not a title or double-barrelled name to be seen.

This Brentwood Grammar School team from 1866 included England unofficial internationals Alexander Nash and RSF Walker, standing either side of the teacher. Brentwood provided a number of prominent early footballers.

As football was confined to six winter months, October to March, it was only natural that players would have alternative activities for the rest of the year. For some, football was not their first or best sport, it was simply a way of keeping fit for the summer. Many were proficient in rowing, athletics and cricket, others in boxing, shooting, canoeing or tennis. Where they do not feature, almost without exception, is in the traditional field sports of hunting and shooting, indicating that this was a new breed of urban sportsmen who wanted to follow healthy pursuits and lead active lives.

The sequence of events which ultimately led to the first international matches can be traced to 1867. Four years after the initial burst of enthusiasm that followed its formation, the FA boasted just ten member clubs[3] and its annual meeting in February attracted only six people. The president, Ebenezer Cobb Morley, said they should seriously consider that night whether it were worthwhile to continue the association or to dissolve it.

According to Robert Graham, who was appointed honorary secretary at that meeting, 'the work of the Association was looked upon with distrust, especially by the public schools, none of which had joined the movement'.[4] The organisation could have foundered had it not taken a series of initiatives which transformed its fortunes.

First, important alterations were made to the laws of the game which aligned them more closely with other kicking games, eliminating handling and touches down, and introducing the stipulation that a goal could only be scored if the ball passed under the tape, instead of at any height. 'It was hoped that these alterations might conciliate many clubs and schools other than those who followed the Rugby game,' Graham recalled, acknowledging that any reconciliation between the codes was now considered impossible: 'The Association decided to throw in its lot entirely with the opponents of Rugby'.

Graham then took on the prodigious task of writing to every known football club in the United Kingdom, inviting them to play according to a universal code: 'Dear Sir, I wish to call your attention to this Association. It has now been in existence for nearly four years, and its rules have had the careful consideration of all the most experienced players in the Metropolis. The result, after many meetings and much patient labour, is that a code of rules has been formed, at once simple and easy of adoption. They are, as far as possible, free from unnecessary danger, yet retaining all that is most scientific and interesting, in all the diversified games that have been in vogue.'

His sales talk had such a positive response that by the end of the year he was able to report an increase in FA membership to 30, including the first public schools, Charterhouse and Westminster, as well as clubs in Yorkshire, Wiltshire and South Wales. Graham was also aware from his correspondence that numerous other clubs were now subscribing to FA rules, among them Queen's Park in Glasgow.

To celebrate this expansion and to maintain the momentum, a county match, Middlesex v Surrey and Kent, was arranged for 2 November 1867. Although it had to be moved at the last minute to a poor pitch at Battersea Park (permission to use Beaufort House in Walham Green was withdrawn because of a dispute between Lord Ranelagh and the Amateur Athletic Club) it marked a turning point. Association football's first representative football match was praised in *The Field* as 'such a decided success that we may look forward to a series of similar friendly meetings'. Next, Kent played Surrey (12-a-side) at Brompton in January 1868, which had the desired effect of calling further attention to the work of the FA, and these county games can be considered the immediate precursors to the first internationals; they included many of the same players.

Westminster was one of the first public schools to join the Football Association, in 1871 was captained by future England international and FA Cup winner Walpole Vidal, holding the ball. (*image copyright David Rice*)

The following month, conscious that association football needed to continue expanding its reach, Charles Alcock proposed bolstering the FA with 'players of acknowledged repute and influence' who would 'infuse fresh strength into the ranks of the committee'.[5] The committee doubled in size to 12 and, key to the events reported in this book, four of the new recruits considered themselves Scottish and would go on to

14

represent Scotland in the unofficial internationals: James Kirkpatrick (Civil Service), Arthur Kinnaird (Old Etonians), Kenneth Muir Mackenzie (Old Carthusians) and Gilbert Kennedy (Old Harrovians). Already on the FA committee was former secretary Robert Willis, whose father was Scottish.

The infusion of new blood worked well, and by autumn 1868 the press reported that the FA had 'lately shown signs of accessing a vaster field wherein to occupy its sphere of usefulness'.[6] Permission was granted to John Lillywhite to publish the first *Football Annual*, which would be edited by Alcock for many years, and this not only disseminated information about the progress of the game, it also quantified its expansion by listing details of all the clubs.

The final catalyst, which enabled football to become a spectator sport, was the availability of a suitable arena to stage high profile matches. With a fine piece of visionary thinking, Alcock persuaded William Burrup, secretary of Surrey County Cricket Club[7], of the financial advantages of allowing footballers to use Kennington Oval. Just south of the Thames, home of Surrey CCC since the 1840s, the Oval fitted the bill perfectly: it could accommodate thousands of spectators around the flat turf of the cricket outfield. It even had proper dressing rooms for the players.

The first football match at the Oval was Wanderers v West Kent on 9 October 1869, Charles Nepean scoring twice to give the visitors a 2-0 victory. Clubs jumped at the opportunity of using the new venue and soon it hosted games every week.

The Oval offered the potential for something bigger and at the turn of the year someone – unfortunately it is not known who – had a brainwave and suggested a new attraction: a contest between the best footballers of England and Scotland.

The scene was set. International football could begin.

---

[1] FG Wood, *Beeton's Football*, p7.

[2] Cotton duck is a hard-wearing material, similar to canvas.

[3] Barnes, Civil Service, Crystal Palace, Kensington School, London Scottish Rifles, NNs Kilburn, Royal Engineers, Sheffield, Wanderers and Worlabye House.

[4] RG Graham, *The Badminton Magazine*, January 1899, p75-87.

[5] *The Field*, 29 February 1868, reporting the FA annual meeting of 26 February.

[6] *The Field*, 26 September 1868.

[7] Alcock succeeded Burrup as secretary of Surrey CCC in 1872, sealing his own career as a sports administrator

Chapter 2

A LUCKY LONG KICK

March 1870: the first international draws a crowd

HISTORY COULD have been kinder to Robert Crawford. His achievements as a decorated war hero were brushed under the carpet as he ended his life in disgrace, convicted of a brutal murder. His place in Scottish sporting legend, as scorer of football's first international goal, has been forgotten.

His counterpart Alfred Baker, who scored a late equaliser for England, was only slightly more fortunate. He built a business empire before he, too, had an ignominious end, quite literally running out of breath while hurrying to catch a train at Willesden Station.

Both men have virtually vanished from the annals of sport. Yet, on a spring day in 1870, they and their colleagues set the ball rolling for one of the world's greatest sporting phenomena: international football.

Never mind that only a few hundred souls huddled round the ropes to witness the match, this was the start of something big. The concept of two countries playing each other at football created a fervour greater than the Victorian pioneers could ever have imagined. Within a generation, similar contests attracted crowds of 100,000; in the modern era, the World Cup Final is seen on television by almost a billion people.

While many historians point to the pervasive influence of Charles Alcock on the early organisation of football, nobody – not even Alcock himself – has claimed personal credit for the idea of an international match. However, with five of the 12 members of the Football Association committee claiming Scottish heritage, it is not hard to imagine where the suggestion came from.

International sport was not an entirely new concept. There were established England v Scotland contests at cricket[1] and shooting[2] – in fact one of the footballers, Wingfield Malcolm MP, had represented Scotland at shooting the year before. Even in football, a few local matches purported to capture the spirit of international rivalry, the

16

earliest known being staged in 1856 between cadets at the Royal Military Academy in Woolwich, English v Scotch and Irish, 20 a side.[3] However, these games can safely be dismissed from having any direct relevance to the events of 1870.

The first intimation in the press was a note in *The Field* on 22 January 1870: 'A match between the leading representatives of the Scotch and English sections will be played at the Oval on Saturday the 19th February next, under the auspices of the Association.'[4] There were instructions for players who were 'duly qualified and desirous of assisting either party' to communicate with Charles Alcock or Robert Graham for English players, and to James Kirkpatrick or Arthur Kinnaird for the Scotch (as the advert put it). These team selectors were all FA committee members, with Alcock about to take over from Graham as the Association's secretary; while Kirkpatrick and Kinnaird, although born in Canada and London respectively, came from Scottish families and were among the game's leading players.

The recruitment message was repeated two weeks later in *The Sportsman*, a newspaper which gave prominent coverage to football and, conveniently, counted Alcock among its staff; curiously, however, it was not submitted to the other leading sports paper, *Bell's Life* (not even for their weekly fixture list), which probably explains their dismissive comments on the game itself.

It is not known how many players responded to the appeal, but being an entirely London-based affair, Alcock and Graham had the easier task to make up a team of their countrymen whose playing abilities were well known. In fact, Alcock did not have to look further than his own club to assess the talent available: every single one of those initially selected for England was a member of Wanderers. Given the relaxed attitude to club membership at the time, most of the players also turned out for other teams, so the line-up as printed in the papers gave the misleading impression that they were drawn from a wide variety of clubs (Alcock, for example, gave his team as Old Harrovians).

As well as Wanderers links, England's players also had a solidly public school background in common. There were four Harrovians (Alcock and Alfred Thornton were old boys, Edward Bowen and Parry Crake were still at the school as teacher and pupil respectively), while Eton supplied Edgar Lubbock, from a great sporting family, and Evelyn Freeth. From Westminster came JC Smith and the youngest participant, 16-year-old Walpole Vidal. Alexander Nash had learned his football at Brentwood Grammar School, an important early nursery of the game, while Thomas Hooman (who later dropped out) was at Charterhouse.

The only 'outsider' at that stage was Baker, the son of a north London property auctioneer. Although he did not have public school credentials – in fact it is uncertain where he went to school – he had been involved in association football right from the start, playing in the Secretary's XIV in 1864.[5] He brought his vibrant personality and sporting talents to the party and was so entrenched in the football establishment he would be trusted with selecting future England teams. He was also very fast, and the following month he won the 100 yards championship at the Amateur Athletic Club.

Kirkpatrick and Kinnaird could not have relished finding eleven Scots who were up to the task, even with a sizeable Scottish community in London. Taking a different approach from the English, they sprang a few surprises by including men who were not regulars on the London football scene, and no Wanderers players (apart from themselves) were in their initial team selection.

Scotland's political defenders: Wingfield Malcolm MP and Willy Gladstone MP

Their masterstroke was unique in the history of football – the parliamentary defence. Two Old Etonian members of parliament, WH Gladstone and JW Malcolm, were giants among men, and would prove an almost insurmountable barrier for the English forwards. Wingfield Malcolm, whose parliamentary seat was in Lincolnshire, was 36 years old but still an active sportsman and presented an intimidating figure at 6 feet 5 inches, with girth to match and a ferocious beard. One report commented that 'like Agamemnon of old, [he] towered over his antagonists and helpmates'. Willy Gladstone, MP for Whitby and eldest son of the Prime Minister, was almost as tall, and although he had not played football for years he had a fearsome reputation from his Eton days. His major passion was for choral hymn music, but there was no choir-boy about his play.

For the rest of the Scotland team, Kirkpatrick, a clerk in the Admiralty, took advantage of the Civil Service's tendency to employ Scots by inviting the Baillie-Hamilton brothers (Colonial Office and Treasury), William Lindsay (India Office) and RRN Ferguson (Treasury)[6]. The eleven was completed by Kenneth Muir Mackenzie, a young lawyer who had been captain of football at Charterhouse, Harrow schoolboy Robert Crawford, and Lord Kilmarnock (Charles Gore Hay, son of the Earl of Erroll), who had been in the Harrow football eleven a couple of years before.

It was quite an achievement to put together a Scotland side in London, but a myth grew that the players' Scottish links were tenuous in the extreme, such as having gone shooting in the Highlands, or a fondness for whisky. One commentator wrote: 'The qualification being a Scotch name, so that any 'Mac' who could at all shape well was almost certain of election.'[7] In later years even Alcock called it a 'counterfeit' and wrote: 'It was a poor imitation of the genuine article, as the Scotchmen were in some cases merely Scotch residents in London, while a few had no better qualification than Scotch extraction – some even hardly had this claim.'[8]

However, while some later Scotland recruits were indeed suspect, the evidence for this first international does not bear out these claims. Although only Muir Mackenzie had been born north of the border, Kinnaird and Kirkpatrick's original selection all had genuine Scottish heritage, with parents or grandparents born north of the border. In fact, they would have qualified for Scotland under modern regulations, which allow for eligibility based on birth back to grandparent level. They even displayed the unfortunate Scottish characteristic of taking the lead against the run of play only to have victory snatched from their grasp by a last minute equaliser, thereby setting the tone of anguish for future generations of the Tartan Army.

All was set for the match on 19 February until a severe frost intervened: it was so cold that the Thames was full of floating blocks of ice and the playing surface of the Oval was rock solid. While it was not unusual for football to be played in atrocious conditions, the risk of breaking bones on frozen earth was deemed too great for gentlemen who had to go to work on the Monday. There was no alternative but to put the game back a couple of weeks.

Numerous other sporting events fell victim to the weather that week, and when Oxford University sports were postponed, the students staged a two mile skating race around Port Meadow which was 'won' by Frederick Chappell (a man whose name will appear regularly in this book); he was then disqualified for not going the full distance.

The following Wednesday, the FA held its annual meeting, at which Alcock was elected honorary secretary and treasurer. A report of the meeting looked forward to the international and noted that 'The English *train* will be composed of representatives of Westminster School, Charterhouse, Old Etonians, Old Harrovians, and Crystal Palace, Barnes, Clapham Rovers and NNs clubs.' (There was no mention of Wanderers.) The committee also continued the development of the laws of the game by introducing the concept of a half-time interval and change of ends if no goals had been scored by then – although ends would continue to be changed after every goal – and decreed that 'handling of the ball under any pretence whatever shall be prohibited'.

Because of the postponement, the team selections had to be amended. For England, Hooman was replaced by WC Butler of Barnes, a civil servant who did not have a Wanderers membership. Scotland's Lord Kilmarnock was required for duty with the Royal Horse Guards, and his place was taken by civil servant George Gordon (Queen's Bench Office); then Ferguson called off at the eleventh hour, to be replaced by Alexander Morten, a veteran who played in goal and brought the combined age of the three man defence up to 108. There were also reports that Charles Nepean of Oxford University and Lieutenant CH Johnston[9] of Royal Engineers were considered for selection by Scotland, but neither were available.

It was clear the footballing public, such as it was, was intrigued by the prospect of international competition and on Saturday 5 March 1870 there was an unexpectedly large crowd at the Oval, 'the entire limit of the ground being lined by an enthusiastic array of the supporters of both sides'. This was estimated at 500-600 people, not a big crowd by modern standards, but much more than football was accustomed to.

England's team was listed in alphabetical order, with the happy coincidence that Alcock, at the top of the list, was team captain, a position he retained in all five unofficial internationals. It has not been possible to ascertain the full tactical formation of either team, although it was likely to have been eight forwards with a half-back, back and goalkeeper. None of the newspaper reports mention an umpire, which indicates that any disputes were settled between the captains.

Kirkpatrick won the toss and chose to play with the biting wind behind Scotland, while Alcock had the honour of kicking-off at about quarter past three. On a ground that was slippery because of overnight rain, the teams were well balanced but most people expected England to win. Indeed, they had most of the pressure in the first half, but the Scottish defence worked well together with Gladstone, in particular, showing he had lost none of his skill.

After 45 minutes there was no score and the sides changed ends according to the new rule, although there was no interval. As Alcock became exasperated by the lack of goals, he decided to be more adventurous and called his goalkeeper upfield to bolster the attack.[10] The identity of the goalkeeper has never been established, but the tactic had disastrous consequences: with all the England players engaged at one end of the pitch, the ball broke free and was chased upfield by Scotland's youngest player, 17-year-old Robert Crawford. Finding no-one in his way, he punted the ball in the direction of goal and his accurate shot from distance, also described as 'a lucky long kick'[11], rolled over the line to give the Scots the lead with just 15 minutes to play. It was 'hailed with tremendous cheers, the partisans of the Scotch being apparently almost overpowered with joy'.

The sides changed ends again, restoring the benefit of the wind to Scotland. As the English tried with increasing desperation to get back on level terms, the Scots held firm against their onslaught but just as it looked like they would see the match out, Alfred Baker found a path through their defence 'by one of the finest runs that have ever been witnessed' and fired home the equaliser. A few seconds later time was called and the world's first football international ended in a 1-1 draw.

The interest generated by the contest was immense. For the first time, a report of a football match in London played under association rules reached the attention of Scottish readers; there was even a report in the Australian press, although it took over two months to reach the far side of the world. Not everyone was happy, however, and *Bell's Life* – normally very supportive of football – allocated just one paragraph and dismissed the game: 'Although the title would lead many persons to fancy that this was an international affair, it can hardly be described as such, since it is merely a meeting of certain members of the clubs who play Association rules, and these are divided into two teams, as they hail North or South of the Tweed.' The paper also squeezed in a dig at Alcock: 'had the English captain been a trifle more careful in his generalship, the victory would, in our opinion, have rested with his side by a goal to none'.

Despite these sour grapes, elsewhere the event was hailed a success and there was soon a demand for a rematch. As it was too late for a further game that season, the FA announced in the summer that two more internationals had been scheduled for the following season. It was a promising start.

5 March 1870: first unofficial international
ENGLAND 1 (Baker), SCOTLAND 1 (Crawford)
Kennington Oval, London

England	*Scotland*
CW Alcock (Old Harrovians, capt)	J Kirkpatrick (Civil Service, capt)
AJ Baker (No Names)	AF Kinnaird (Crusaders)
EE Bowen (Wanderers)	WH Gladstone (Old Etonians) *back*
WC Butler (Barnes)	REW Crawford (Harrow)
WP Crake (Harrow)	CRB Hamilton (Civil Service)
E Freeth (Civil Service) *back*	WAB Hamilton (Old Harrovians)
E Lubbock (Old Etonians) *back*	W Lindsay (Old Wykehamists)
A Nash (Clapham Rovers)	JW Malcolm (London Scottish Rifles) *back*
JC Smith (Crusaders)	KA Muir Mackenzie (Old Carthusians)
AH Thornton (Old Harrovians)	GC Gordon (No Names)
RWS Vidal (Westminster)	A Morten (Crystal Palace) *goalkeeper*

MATCH REPORT
Glasgow Herald

No better proof can be adduced of the extensive popularity enjoyed by the game of football in the vicinity of London, and indeed in all the southern districts of England, than the intense interest to which the preliminaries incidental to the arrangement of the great International Football Match, which was decided on the ground of the County of Surrey Cricket Club, at Kennington Oval, on Saturday last, gave rise. For weeks prior to the original fixture, the members of the various clubs situated in the neighbourhood of the English metropolis had been on the alert to glean any authoritative news on the subject of the players who had been selected to do battle for the interests of the two countries; and when, owing to the severity of the frost, which rendered the ground dangerously unfit for play on Saturday 19 February, a postponement of a fortnight was thus necessitated, the delay only intensified the excitement, producing an assemblage of spectators at the Oval such as is rarely seen on the occasion of a football match.

By way of explanation it is necessary to state that the settlement of the contest is entirely due to the energy of the committee of the Football Association, which body has worked seriously and untiringly to secure the extension of football, and with no little purpose; and it will also be requisite to state that the rules of the association, which governed the present match, are in every important feature opposed to the principles of the Rugby game, as adopted in Scotland, running with the ball, and the other specialities of the laws promulgated by Rugbeians being strictly prohibited by the English legislators of football, who allow no one to touch the ball with his hands except the goal-keeper, and this only when in defence of the goal.

The weather was exceptionally fine after the heavy rains of the two previous days and the ground, though somewhat slippery, was not as heavy as had been anticipated. Both countries, it is due to the respective captains to state, were most ably represented, Scotland especially mustering in the ranks of its army many whose names are familiar to and honoured in football circles as well as in more important and weighty scenes of life.

Shortly after three o'clock all the necessary preliminaries having been arranged, and the choice of goals having fallen to the lot of the Northerners, the ball was kicked off by the captain of the English party, the latter having to face a wind of no inconsiderable force. Thus opposed, the Southrons during the earlier part of the game were able to make but little progress, although several rushes on the part of Messrs CW Alcock and A Baker would undoubtedly have been crowned with success but for the excellent back play shown by Messrs WH Gladstone and A Morten, the former of whom, though rather out of practice, fully proved that his foot had not lost the cunning for which it was famed only a few years back when doing battle on behalf of the Eton College Eleven.

During the first portion of the game no score was achieved by either of the two nations and consequently after the lapse of the first period of three quarters of an hour the positions of the two sides were reversed, the English now in their turn being able to claim all the advantages incidental to the aid of a propitious wind. The Scottish Eleven were now closely assailed in their own quarters, and on several occasions their goal was so closely besieged by the pressing attacks of the enemy as to be placed in the most imminent peril, Messrs Baker, Butler and Nash signalling themselves out for special notice among those who approached the immediate neighbourhood of their adversaries' goal. In this manner the play continued with but little variety, the Englishmen never allowing their rivals to raise the siege until a general run up by the latter brought the ball in to the vicinity of the English posts, and a lucky long kick by Mr RE Crawford, in the reprehensible absence of England's goalkeeper, placed a goal to the account of Scotland, amid vociferous applause from the 'canny Scots', who represented no small portion of the spectators.

After a further reversal of positions, the English division, nettled at the ill luck that had attended their efforts, played up with the greatest energy and determination, and after one good attempt by Mr E Freeth had only been frustrated by the excellent defence of the opposition, Mr A Baker, by one of the finest runs that have ever been witnessed, landed the ball in the heart of the Scottish goal, to the enthusiastic plaudits of the spectators, the match thus terminating in a drawn game, with one goal to each nation, and England only averting defeat in the space of one minute.

---

[1] A cricket match between All England and 22 of Scotland was first played in Edinburgh in 1849 and became an annual event.

[2] The Elcho Shield, between the best shots in the Volunteer movement, was first contested in 1862 between England and Scotland. It is still an annual competition today.

[3] *Bells Life*, 19 October 1856; they repeated the game the following year, and in 1860 an 'annual match' of English v Scotch & Irish was staged at Sandhurst.

[4] To add to the international flavour, the same edition of *The Field* reported that a football club had been formed in Le Havre, just across the channel in France.

[5] The inaugural match played under Football Association rules was at Battersea Park on 9 January 1864, an FA President's select against an FA Secretary's team, 14-a-side.

[6] Robert Ronald Norman Ferguson, an Etonian, would not play for Scotland although his younger brother Harold did so twice, in 1871-72.

[7] Old International, *25 Years Football*, p25

[8] CW Alcock, Association Football, *The English Illustrated Magazine*, 1891, p285

[9] Currell Halliday Johnston (1849-1879) was educated at Cheltenham College. The son of a soldier from Dumfries, he was born in France and died in Italy.

[10] Sending the goalkeeper upfield, to be fair, was not an unusual ploy; another high profile instance was the FA Cup Final of 1873 when Oxford University tried it, with similar results.

[11] *The Field* went further: 'a rather fluky long kick by RE Crawford securing a lucky goal for the Scottish eleven'.

Chapter 3

AN UNEXPECTED OUTCOME

1870-71: the catalyst for the first rugby international

CHARLES ALCOCK acknowledged that it was a disadvantage for the first representative match to feature only Scots living in London and knew the FA had to deflect some criticism over its parochial nature. As the 1870-71 season opened, he wrote to *The Field*: 'The committee are desirous of making the matches annual fixtures of importance by investing them with more than local interest, and at the same time are especially anxious to infuse into the contests something of an international character.'[1]

How to achieve this was still not clear. Alcock was aware that association football was very much in the minority north of the border, where rugby dominated, and this was compounded by the time and expense of travelling from Glasgow or Edinburgh to London for a match. Undaunted, he placed notices in the London sporting press, inviting nominations for players to be sent to Kirkpatrick or Kinnaird for the Scots, and to Baker or himself for the English.[2] He also wrote more fulsomely to the Scottish press: 'It is the object of the committee to select the best elevens at their disposal in the two countries, and I cannot but think that the appearance of some of the more prominent celebrities of football on the northern side of the Tweed would do much to disseminate a healthy feeling of good fellowship among the contestants.'[3]

Much to his relief, this appeal struck a chord at virtually the only football club in Scotland to have adopted the association game. The members of Queen's Park, formed in 1867 on the south side of Glasgow, were intrigued by the prospect of closer links with the FA as a means of ending their isolated status, but equally were daunted by the cost of sending players to London. Their solution, for now, was to nominate Robert Smith, who had moved to the capital and was playing for South Norwood, while retaining his membership of Queen's Park.

25

Alcock's prayers had been answered: the Scotland team for the second match would include someone who had actually played football in Scotland. It was a good call in more ways than one, as Smith went on to have a crucial role in developing the links between the FA and Scottish clubs, effectively becoming the voice of Scottish football in London.

The FA's problems, however, were far from over, as rugby football would soon seize the initiative. Alcock could hardly have imagined that his efforts to broaden the scope of the Scotland football team would lead directly to the establishment of the Rugby Football Union, and to rugby taking the lead as a truly international sport.

In the meantime, his efforts were devoted to ensuring the English could put together the strongest possible side, and he chaired a selection committee of team captains. They included AJ Baker (Wanderers), D Allport (Crystal Palace), RH Birkett (Clapham Rovers), M Jutsum (Upton Park), JP Tatham (Hampstead Heathens), JH Giffard (Civil Service), PPV Turner (CCC), J Cockerell (Brixton), MP Betts (West Kent) and RW Willis (Barnes).[4]

They had 28 aspiring players to choose from, and nine of the selectors met on the Monday before the game (Betts voted by proxy while Willis was unable to attend). After their deliberations, three (Alcock, Baker and Cockerell) took advantage of the opportunity to list themselves in the team, while Crake, Lubbock and Vidal were retained from the first game. RSF Walker of Clapham Rovers (who had been playing rugby for Sandhurst on the day of the first international) was brought in and there were four youthful recruits still at school – TN Carter (captain of the Eton field eleven), WB Paton (captain of the Harrow eleven), HJ Preston (Eton) and RWS Vidal (Westminster).

Among those who did not make it into the side were HJ Lake and SR Tatham of Hampstead Heathens, CC Harvey of Crystal Palace, Charterhouse schoolboy HS King, and the first two northern players to get a mention, EE Royds of Rochdale (father of future England rugby international Sir Percy Royds) and WB Harrop of Sheffield Garrick Club.[5]

Meanwhile, Kirkpatrick and Kinnaird sifted through a much shorter list of potential candidates for Scotland, and were 'greatly crippled by the comparatively small selection of players at [their] disposal'.[6] While their own names were first on the teamsheet, the only others they could call upon from the previous season's match were Robert Crawford (still at school) and William Lindsay. WH Gladstone

26

sent his apologies and, as stated, Robert Smith was nominated by Queen's Park, so six more newcomers had to be found.

A place went to Scots-born civil servant Galfrid Congreve, listed as an Old Rugbeian although he had not attended Rugby School – it was probably a reference to his preference for rugby football, as he focused entirely on the oval ball thereafter with Ravenscourt Park. Others had a more tenuous connection to Scotland: Quintin Hogg and Gilbert Kennedy could at least claim to come from ancient (although long-departed) Scottish families, but Charles Nepean's inclusion appears to be due to his cousin having married a Scot.[7]

The final two selections provoked a fraught build-up to kick-off. On the morning of the match, John Inglis of Charterhouse (of whom, more later) was refused permission to play by his school and his place was taken by Henry Primrose, born near Edinburgh on the estate of his grandfather, Lord Rosebery, and educated at Glenalmond. Then, when William Baillie-Hamilton simply did not turn up, a frantic last-minute search for a substitute came up with W Bailey (Civil Service), whose name is spelled Baillie in some reports. His identity is not immediately obvious but the only contemporary footballer who fits the bill was William Heap Bailey, who had captained Upton Park. He could allude to a Scottish connection thanks to a family tradition that an ancestor had come south with Bonnie Prince Charlie's Jacobite army in 1745 and settled in his home town of Derby.

While the Scots conducted this search, the England eleven had time to pose for a photograph, although regrettably no copies are known to have survived.[8]

The match attracted about six hundred spectators, 'an array so large as to leave hardly a vacant place in the line of ropes which bounded the ground'. Two umpires were appointed and they gave the signal as, in perfect conditions, Nepean kicked off punctually at three o'clock. Not surprisingly, Scotland took time to settle and after about 20 minutes the English went ahead: Alcock dribbled to the goal line and his centre was met by Walker, who kicked the ball into the Scottish goal past the despairing Kirkpatrick. Ends were changed, but England maintained the upper hand and came close to a second as an Alcock shot hit the outside of the post, then Baker had a goal disallowed.

Scotland were further handicapped by an injury to Hogg, who was 'so lame as to render the least exertion painful,' and the team made little headway: 'on several occasions [they] pierced the first lines of the English, but in each case were driven back before they had reached the

27

inner circle defended by the opposition backs.' As the game entered its final stages the Scots were 'incited to desperation by the thought of the defeat that appeared imminent,' but their efforts were in vain and it finished 1-0.

19 November 1870: unofficial match 2
ENGLAND 1 (Walker), SCOTLAND 0
Kennington Oval, London

England	Scotland
CW Alcock (Harrow Pilgrims, capt)	J Kirkpatrick (Civil Service, capt) *gk*
AJ Baker (Wanderers)	AF Kinnaird (Old Etonians) *back*
TN Carter (Eton College) *back*	REW Crawford (Harrow)
J Cockerell (Brixton Club) *back*	HW Primrose (Civil Service)
WP Crake (Barnes Club)	CEB Nepean (Univ College, Oxford) *back*
TC Hooman (Wanderers)	Q Hogg (Wanderers) back
E Lubbock (West Kent) back	W Lindsay (Rochester Club)
WB Paton (Harrow)	GF Congreve (Old Rugbeian)
HE Preston (Eton College)	R Smith (Queen's Park)
RWS Vidal (Westminster)	WH Bailey (Civil Service)
RSF Walker (Clapham Rovers)	GG Kennedy (Wanderers)

Umpires: MP Betts (for England) and A Morten (for Scotland)

MATCH REPORT
Sporting Gazette

Saturday's great match commenced at three o'clock, the Scotch at the last moment being deprived of the assistance of Messrs JF Inglis (Charterhouse) and WB Hamilton (Civil Service) but two substitutes were found in Messrs [H]W Primrose and W Baillie (Civil Service). After the northerners had kept their opponents at bay for some time, Mr Alcock made a splendid run from the centre of the ground and being cleverly supported by Mr Walker, a goal was obtained – the successful kick being made by the latter, and it was the only one made throughout the game. Ends being changed, Mr Baker made a good attempt to reach the Scotch goal, but failed in effecting a twist when within a few yards of it. The ball was soon after retained in the middle of the grounds, and the Scotch team pressing their opponents, the match became very exciting, the lines of Scotland being afterwards menaced by the energetic rushes of England, who were successfully repulsed by Messrs Nepean, Hogg and Kinnaird, who played admirably as backs; for although Mr Hogg was slightly lame, he was formidable in opposition. Thus the game progressed and most evenly; for while those named were most indefatigable in

28

their endeavours to lower the English goal, Messrs Alcock, Vidal, Cockerell, Baker and Hooman were equally so in trying successfully to send the ball through the Scotch lines. At one time Mr Kirkpatrick got the ball down to the English goal by a fine exhibition of dribbling, and for a time England seemed in imminent danger of losing the only advantage that had been gained. To protect their goal the Englishmen rushed en masse on their opponents, and after some more fine play succeeded in bringing the ball away to the other end of the field, where the captain of the English team in quick succession made two brilliant attempts to reduce the Scotch lines, the first failing on account of the ball glancing outwards from one of the posts. Mr Hooman also got the ball in near the Scotch goal, and Mr Baker having brought it to bear, at once drove it under the line, but it was disallowed. Mr Cockerell made some good runs.

When the report of England's victory appeared in the Scottish press, events took an entirely unexpected turn, initially prompted by this condemnation from a correspondent to *The Scotsman* who identified himself only as 'S': 'It must not be supposed that the eleven who represented us have in their defeat involved our national reputation as athletes.'

Alcock was forced to respond in defence of the validity of the match: 'I must join issue with your correspondent in some instances. First, I assert that of whatever the Scotch eleven may have been composed, the right to play was open to every Scotchman whether his lines were cast North or South of the Tweed and that if in the face of the invitations publicly given through the columns of leading journals of Scotland the representative eleven consisted chiefly of Anglo-Scotians ... the fault lies on the heads of the players of the north, not on the management who sought the services of all alike impartially. To call the team London Scotchmen contributes nothing. The match was, as announced, to all intents and purposes between England and Scotland.'9

In an attempt at conciliation, he suggested England could play against a team of Scots-based players, with a cup and medals at stake, but made a stipulation: 'More than eleven we do not care to play as with greater numbers it is our opinion that the game becomes less scientific and more a trial of charging and brute force.'

This offhand accusation was a red rag to a bull. Rugby football had been played in Scotland by the major schools since the 1850s, and carried on into the universities. In 1870 there were at least ten established clubs playing the carrying code, including Edinburgh Academicals, Glasgow Academicals, Royal High School Former Pupils,

Merchistonians, Edinburgh University, Glasgow University, St Andrews University and independent (open) clubs including West of Scotland, Edinburgh Wanderers and Perthshire.

The Scotsman published another riposte, this time from 'HM' (thought to be Hely Hutchinson Almond, Head Master of Loretto), with the colourful allusion that the association game is to rugby football 'as moonlight unto sunlight and as water unto wine'. The anonymous 'S' then pitched in with some more rambling views, backing the suggestion of an international but describing association football as 'a modification of the great parent code, with the more violent features expurged'.

While this exchange of letters was going on, a lot of talking was taking place behind the scenes. Glasgow Academicals had played host to Merchistonians on 26 November and a week later the Merchistonians were at Raeburn Place to take on Edinburgh Academicals. The team captains (John Arthur, Benjamin Hall Blyth and Francis Moncreiff) took the opportunity to discuss the issue and mooted the idea of a challenge to England to play a football international under rugby rules. They sought and received support from other club captains, and together they penned a letter, dated 6 December, laying down the gauntlet to the English:

'There is a pretty general feeling among Scotch football players that the football power of the old country was not properly represented in the late so-called International Football Match. Not that we think the play of the gentlemen who represented Scotland otherwise than very good – for that it was so is amply proved by the stout resistance they offered to their opponents and by the fact that they were beaten by only one goal – but that we consider the Association rules, in accordance with which the late game was played, not such as to bring together the best team Scotland could turn out.

'With a view of really testing what Scotland could do against an English team, we, as representing the football interests of Scotland, hereby challenge any team selected from the whole of England to play us a match, twenty-a-side – Rugby rules.'

As well as Arthur, Hall Blyth and Moncreiff, the signatories were Alexander Hamilton Robertson (captain of West of Scotland) and John Henry Oatts (captain of St Salvator FC, a college at St Andrews University). Published in *The Scotsman, Bell's Life* and *The Field*, their defiant claim to represent Scottish football was not just a rebuff to Queen's Park, it was a godsend to the rugby-playing teams in London, and in particular to Blackheath, who had caused so much discord by walking away from the Football Association in 1863. Frederic Stokes, captain of Blackheath, was deputed to open negotiations for an England side to travel to Edinburgh in the spring; conveniently, his club secretary was Benjamin Burns, who had learned his football at Edinburgh Academy. Even before the match was arranged, cross-border contact was established as Glasgow Academicals became the first Scottish football team of any code to travel to England, playing (and winning) matches in Liverpool and Manchester on 16 and 17 December.

To prepare for the international, the rugby clubs formed the Rugby Football Union, whose inaugural meeting was held on 26 January 1871 at the Pall Mall Restaurant in Cockspur Street (just across the road from Arthur Kinnaird's house in Pall Mall East).[10] There was no equivalent body in Scotland, for either football code, until 1873.

While this was going on, association football was not standing still, and a South v North match, played in December at the Oval, featured a number of provincial footballers in London for the first time, the North including players from Nottingham, Sheffield, Newark and Liverpool (as well as three Londoners – Kinnaird, Hogg and Nepean – who gave their 'place of origin' as Scotland).

Alcock wrote again to the *Glasgow Herald* to try and drum up support in Scotland: 'In order to give ample time to enable Scotch players desirous of representing their country to make the necessary preparations, I request the favour of a few lines in your paper to notify to all concerned that the second of the two international matches fixed for the present season will take place in London. The rules of the Football Association will, as before, be enforced; and, on behalf of the committee, I earnestly request the co-operation of the steadily increasing army of Scotchmen who follow their laws.'[11]

There is no indication that his letter provoked any additional responses for team selectors Kinnaird and Hogg to consider, and they opted for another London-based eleven. Things appeared to be looking up as Kirkpatrick, Lindsay, Nepean and Robert Smith retained their places, Gladstone was again available, and Inglis was this time given permission by his school to take part. Another newcomer was Oxford student Arnold Kirke Smith, who had a Scottish grandfather (but would be a future England international *against* Scotland in 1872).

However, come 25 February, hopes that the Scots could avoid the match-day panic of last time were dashed. William Baillie-Hamilton

31

again dropped out on the day of the game, and was replaced by Gilbert Primrose[12], whose older brother Henry had played for Scotland in the previous international. Robert Crawford was another late call-off and his place was given to a man reported in the press as F McLean (alternatively Maclean, McClew or McClean) of University College, Oxford.

Not only was there no-one of this name at Oxford at that time, his name is in inverted commas in *The Sportsman*, indicating an alias. It turned out to be a pseudonym for Brasenose College student Frederick Chappell[13], probably to cover up the fact that he had no Scottish connections (he was another future England international, and to confuse matters further would later change his name to Frederick Brunning Maddison).

Alcock and his fellow England selectors made just three changes from the autumn match; the schoolboys Carter, Paton and Preston dropped out, Butler returned to the side, and there were two newcomers, Betts and 17-year-old CW Stephenson. The latter, of Westminster School, had recently been elected to the FA committee, probably its youngest ever member.

The match, as usual, was played at Kennington Oval, in front of five or six hundred spectators whose 'partisanship ran high', and was overseen not only by two umpires but also, for the first time, a referee. Scotland captain Arthur Kinnaird won the toss, choosing to take the backing of the strong wind, and an early series of attacks ended with Nepean 'by some clever execution' putting his side ahead after about 20 minutes. However, this meant that ends were changed and it was England's turn to have the wind.

Gradually they gained the upper hand and ultimately a three-pronged attack ended in Walker shooting just inside the post to grab the equaliser. Both sides made tactical changes, with Cockerell and Betts alternating as goalkeepers for England, Kirkpatrick and Robert Smith doing likewise for Scotland, but it was to no avail and the game ended in a 1-1 draw.

25 February 1871: unofficial match 3
ENGLAND 1 (Walker), SCOTLAND 1 (Nepean)
Kennington Oval, London

England	*Scotland*
CW Alcock (Harrow Pilgrims, capt)	AF Kinnaird (Wanderers, capt)[14]
AJ Baker (Wanderers)	F Chappell (Oxford University)
MP Betts (West Kent) *goalkeeper 1*	WH Gladstone (Old Etonians) *back*
WC Butler (Civil Service)	Q Hogg (Wanderers) *half-back*
J Cockerell (Brixton) *goalkeeper 2*	JF Inglis (Charterhouse)
WP Crake (Barnes)	J Kirkpatrick (Civil Service) *goalkeeper 1*
TC Hooman (Wanderers)	W Lindsay (Old Wykehamist)
E Lubbock (West Kent) *half-back*	CEB Nepean (University College, Oxford)
CW Stephenson (Westminster) *back*	AK Smith (University College, Oxford)
RWS Vidal (Westminster)	R Smith (Queen's Park) *goalkeeper 2*
RSF Walker (Clapham Rovers)	GE Primrose (Civil Service)

Umpires: R Barker (Hertfordshire Rangers, for England)
and W Wallace (Wanderers, for Scotland).
Referee: CM Tebbut (Wanderers)[15]

MATCH REPORT
Bell's Life

*Scotland won the toss, and the ball was kicked off at 3.30 on behalf of
England by Baker, the northerners having a strong wind in their favour, a
decided advantage. From the first the play was most vigorously maintained
by both sides, and each goal was on several occasions seriously menaced, the
honours being equally divided, matters going on in this way for about a
quarter of an hour, when the fine forward play of some members of the Scotch
team began to tell upon their adversaries and the ball was kept in close
proximity to their goal, which shortly after Nepean, by some clever execution,
succeeded in reducing. The ends were then changed, and England derived the
advantage of the strong breeze which prevailed, and they renewed the fight
with increased vigour, which caused the territory of the Scotch side to be
repeatedly invaded, but principally owing to the fine back play of Gladstone
and Hogg the energetic attacks of England were frustrated for upwards of
half an hour, when Butler, Alcock and Walker brought the ball down, the
latter by a well-executed and clever kick sending the ball between the posts,
and the sides were once again on an equality.*

33

By now, preparations were well under way for the first international rugby match, which took place in Edinburgh on 27 March 1871, beating the association players by a year and a half. Benjamin Hall Blyth, captain of Merchistonians, was put in charge of organising the game but planning was not as straightforward as it could have been, as the English went back on an initial agreement to play 15-a-side, and in mid-March intimated that they would in fact be bringing 20 players. There were also arguments about how to determine eligibility, with the Scots insisting on a birth qualification rather than residence; they were concerned about losing players who were at Oxbridge or worked down south, such as Andrew Colville. It worked in his case as he opted for the land of his birth, but there were still exceptions: Benjamin Burns, born and raised in Scotland, had 'gone native' and donned an England shirt, while Northumberland-born Thomas Marshall played for Scotland.

Leaving nothing to chance, the Scots held two trials, in Glasgow and Edinburgh, before settling on a team. One of the players, Robert Irvine, later recalled: 'The men were requested to get into training, and did it. We were ignorant what team England would bring, of what sort of players they had, and of how they would play; and though assured by Colville, a London Merchistonian – and a rare good forward too – that we would find the size, strength and weight not very materially different from our own, many of us entered that match with a sort of vague fear that some entirely new kind of play would be shown by our opponents and that they would out-manoeuvre us entirely.'[16]

The English, on the other hand, had no trial and met in a pub, the Princess of Wales, headquarters of Blackheath, to decide their line-up.

Admission was set at a shilling and a crowd of four thousand crammed into Raeburn Place, the home of Edinburgh Academicals, exceeding all expectations. They were rewarded – unlike in any of the early association football internationals – with a victory for Scotland.

After a scoreless first half, which lasted 50 minutes, Scotland made the breakthrough thanks to an almighty push by the mass of forwards which allowed Buchanan to ground the ball near the touchline. Cross converted the kick to score a goal, which was not as difficult as it could have been, with a narrow pitch and the wind behind him. England replied when Birkett ran wide to score a try, but this time the conversion attempt failed. Scotland managed to increase the margin of victory near the end when Cross touched down, and although he missed the conversion it was of little consequence as the game was almost over. Both Scotland tries were loudly protested by the English, but home umpire HH Almond disagreed and in schoolmasterly fashion he later explained: 'I must say that when an umpire is in doubt, I think he is justified in deciding against the side which makes most noise.'

Having promised to defend their record in London the following season, the Scots celebrated their success by hanging the match ball in the window of a nearby shop 'adorned with ribbons like the tail of a Clydesdale stallion'.[17]

27 March 1871: first rugby football international
SCOTLAND one goal and one try, ENGLAND one try
Raeburn Place, Edinburgh

Scotland	England
T Chalmers (Glasgow Acads)	A Lyon (Liverpool)
WD Brown (Glasgow Acads)	RR Osborne (Manchester)
A Clunies-Ross (St Andrews Univ)	AG Guillemard (West Kent)
TR Marshall (Edinburgh Acads)	W MacLaren (Manchester)
JW Arthur (Glasgow Acads)	JE Bentley (Gipsies)
W Cross (Merchistonians)	F Tobin (Liverpool)
FJ Moncreiff (Edinburgh Acads, capt)	JF Green (West Kent)
JF Finlay (Edinburgh Acads)	F Stokes (Blackheath, capt)
RW Irvine (Edinburgh Acads)	CA Crompton (Blackheath)
J Mein (Edinburgh Acads)	CW Sherrard (Blackheath)
D Drew (Glasgow Acads)	AS Gibson (Manchester)
WJC Lyall (Edinburgh Acads)	HJC Turner (Manchester)
AG Colville (Merchistonians)	J Luscombe (Gipsies)
JS Thomson (Glasgow Acads)	DP Turner (Richmond)
G Ritchie (Merchistonians)	JH Clayton (Liverpool)
W Forsyth (Edinburgh Univ)	A Davenport (Ravenscourt Park)
AH Robertson (West of Scotland)	JM Dugdale (Ravenscourt Park)
R Munro (St Andrews Univ)	AStG Hamersley (Marlborough Nomads)
A Buchanan (Royal High School FP)	BH Burns (Blackheath)
JLH McFarlane (Edinburgh Univ)	RH Birkett (Clapham Rovers)

Umpires: HH Almond (Scotland) and A Ward (England)

MATCH REPORT
Glasgow Herald

This great football match was played yesterday, on the Academy Cricket Ground, Edinburgh, with a result most gratifying for Scotland. The weather was fine and there was a very large turnout of spectators. The competitors

35

were dressed in appropriate costumes, the English wearing a white jersey, ornamented by a red rose, and the Scotch a brown [sic] jersey, with a thistle. Although the good wishes of the spectators went with the Scotch team, yet it was considered that their chance was poor. The difference between the two teams was very marked, the English being of a much heavier and stronger build compared to their opponents. The game commenced shortly after three o'clock, the Scotch getting the kick off, and for a time neither side had any advantage. The Scotch, however, succeeded in driving the ball close to the English goal and, pushing splendidly forward, eventually put it into their opponents' quarters, who, however, prevented any harm accruing by smartly 'touching down'. This result warmed the Englishmen up to their work, and in spite of tremendous opposition they got near the Scotch goal, and kicked the ball past it, but as it was cleverly 'touched down' they got no advantage. This finished the first 50 minutes and the teams changed sides. For a considerable time after the change the ball was sent from side to side, and the 'backs' got more work to do. By some lucky runs, however, the Scotch got on to the borders of the English land, and tried to force the ball past the goal. The English strenuously opposed this attempt, and for a time the struggle was terrible, ending in the Scotch 'touching down' in their opponents' ground, and becoming entitled to a 'try'. This result was received with cheers, which were more heartily renewed when Cross, to whom the 'kick off' was entrusted, made a beautiful goal. This defeat only stirred up the English to fresh effort and, driving the ball across the field, they managed also to secure a 'try' but unfortunately the man who got the 'kick off' did not allow sufficient windage, and the ball fell short. After this the Scotch became more cautious, and playing well together secured after several attempts a second 'try', but good luck did not attend the 'kick off' and the goal was lost. Time being then declared up the game ceased, the Scotch winning by a goal and a 'try'.

---

[1] *The Field*, 17 September 1870

[2] *The Field*, 29 October 1870

[3] *Glasgow Herald*, 3 November 1870; the same letter appeared in the *Edinburgh Evening Courant*.

[4] Their full names were Alfred Joseph Baker, Douglas Allport, Reginald Halsey Birkett, Millner Jutsum, Joseph Perceval Tatham, John Hardinge Giffard, Percy Pollexfen Vere Turner, John Cockerell, Morton Peto Betts and Robert Watson Willis.

[5] The players were Henry J Lake, Sherman Ralph Tatham, Christopher Charles Harvey, Henry Seymour King, Ernest Edmund Royds and William Brown Harrop.

[6] *The Scotsman*, 21 November 1870

[7] Molyneux Hyde Nepean, 3rd Baronet (1813-95) married Isabella Geils of Dunbartonshire, and lived in Duddingston, Edinburgh.

[8] In Alcock's next letter to the *Glasgow Herald* he invited anyone wishing a souvenir of the November international to write in and purchase a photograph of the England eleven, taken by the London Stereoscopic Company.

[9] *The Scotsman*, 28 November 1870

[10] A stone plaque on the building commemorates the event. Curiously, Charles Alcock had proposed the formation of a rugby association as early as September 1869.

[11] *Glasgow Herald*, 7 January 1871

[12] His initials are given as CE Primrose in newspaper reports, but this is clearly a misprint.

[13] The name F McLean also cropped up in a possible England team in November 1872, again as a pseudonym for Chappell.

[14] The team captains are not explicitly stated in any match reports, but it can be inferred that Alcock and Kinnaird were the captains.

[15] Robert Barker, William Wallace and Charles Mansfield Tebbut.

[16] RW Irvine, writing in Marshall, *Football the Rugby Union Game*, p200

[17] RW Irvine, *op cit*, p202

Chapter 4

FOOTBALL'S WATERSHED YEAR

1871-72: the end of the unofficial contests

PUTTING FAMILY and philanthropy before football, Arthur Kinnaird took the entire season off to visit the charitable missions set up by his mother in India. By going on his travels, one of the greatest footballers of the age missed the creation of the FA Cup and the last of the unofficial internationals. He made up for it in later years, winning five cup winners' medals and a cap for Scotland, but in the meantime the Scottish eleven had to get by without him.

Season 1871-72 was something of a watershed for association football as the inaugural FA Cup competition got under way – thanks to Charles Alcock's inspired suggestion – and the Sheffield v London series began, while the last two unofficial internationals were played before making way for the real thing.

In November's opening clash, England initially had the look of a settled side as Alcock could again call upon Lubbock, Vidal, Walker, Betts and Stephenson. However, for once it was England rather than Scotland who had late difficulties with team selection. Henry Lake of Hampstead Heathens and Thomas Hooman called off in the week of the game, to be replaced by the diminutive Percy Weston and Jarvis Kenrick, who had recently scored the first ever goal in the FA Cup; then Eton College football captain Archibald Ruggles-Brise was ill on the day, allowing Parry Crake to return to the side.

There were two other newcomers. Albert Thompson was listed as representing the Eton Club of Cambridge University even though he had already graduated; in fact he was now playing for Wanderers, with whom he would soon win an FA Cup winner's medal. The final name in the team was Thomas Southey Baker, a triple rowing blue at Oxford and former *victor ludorum* of sport at Lancing school, who was with Clapham Rovers.

James Kirkpatrick, who was also on the organising committee of the FA Cup[1], had the thankless task of selecting a Scotland eleven, which was exacerbated as not only was Kinnaird away, but Quintin Hogg was on an extended honeymoon in America.

The usual newspaper appeal for aspiring international players was published just two weeks before the match, although for a change it attracted some useful recruits for the Scots: two young lieutenants in the Royal Engineers, Henry Renny-Tailyour and Hugh Mitchell, came forward. It was to be a particularly memorable year for the former, as Renny-Tailyour achieved the distinction of representing Scotland at both rugby and association rules in the same season, and would also feature for the Engineers in the first FA Cup final. He was asked by Kirkpatrick to captain the Scotland eleven.

Others who were new to the Scotland team included Harold Ferguson, studying for his army commission at Woolwich, and Edward Elliot, a Harrovian who was later described as a 'truly ponderous' footballer. Lindsay, Nepean and Smith all retained their places and to make up the eleven Robert Crawford, who had travelled overnight from a visit to Edinburgh[2], brought in his younger brother Fitzgerald, who had been doing well with Harrow Chequers.

Mindful of the tendency of players to vanish on match day, Scotland named two reserves, Gilbert Kennedy of Wanderers and James Smith, Robert's younger brother, who was newly arrived in London after four years with Queen's Park. As it happened, neither was called upon and Kennedy acted as umpire.

On a cold but sunny day at the Oval, the crowd was noisy and numerous, according to *Bell's Life*: 'a very large attendance of visitors, more in fact than we have ever yet seen at the famed Surrey ground when football matches have been played ... the teams seemed to have an equal number of adherents, their partisans being pretty equally divided.'

The home supporters were soon cheering two quick goals by Walker, although there were protests from the Scots that the first was offside. The umpires decided the goal was good but 'their opinion was much differed with'; it appears there was no referee this time to hear an appeal. Scotland tried to come back into it, but only towards the end did Renny-Tailyour grab a consolation goal. It was too late to stage a comeback and England had a comfortable, if narrow, victory.

18 November 1871: unofficial match 4
ENGLAND 2 (Walker 2), SCOTLAND 1 (Renny-Tailyour)
Kennington Oval, London

England	*Scotland*
CW Alcock (Wanderers, capt)	HW Renny-Tailyour (RE, capt)
TS Baker (Clapham Rovers)	H Mitchell (Royal Engineers)
E Lubbock (Old Etonians) *half-back*	CEB Nepean (Oxford Uni) *half-back*
CW Stephenson (Wanderers) *goalkeeper*	REW Crawford (Old Harrovian)
AC Thompson (Eton Club, Cambridge) *back*	W Lindsay (Old Wykehamist) *back*
RWS Vidal (Westminster)	HS Ferguson (RMA, Woolwich)
RSF Walker (Clapham Rovers)	FH Crawford (Harrow Chequers)
P Weston (Barnes)	AK Smith (Oxford University)
WP Crake (Harrow Chequers)	J Kirkpatrick (Civil Service)
J Kenrick (Clapham Rovers)	R Smith (South Norwood) *gk*
MP Betts (Harrow Chequers)	EHM Elliot (Harrow Chequers)

Umpires: A Stair (England)[3] and GG Kennedy (Scotland)

MATCH REPORT
Bell's Life

The English captain won the toss, and Lieut Renny-Tailyour kicked the ball from the western goal, the Scotchmen having to face the sun, which was shining most brilliantly. For some time after commencing the game was entirely in favour of the English team, despite the unceasing efforts of the captain, and the Oxonians, who were most energetic in their attempts to keep the ball out of their territory, and although they to a certain extent succeeded, they were at length driven back, and their goal was captured by Walker after a splendid rush, followed by a very fine kick. An appeal of offside was made to the umpires but those gentlemen rejected the appeal and ends were changed accordingly, but a very short time had elapsed ere Walker again brought about a reduction of the Scotch fortress, the ball having been splendidly run down by Weston, making four goals obtained in these contests by the captain of the Clapham Rovers. Again ends were reversed, and the Scotchmen, evidently stung by their reverses, were stimulated to greater exertions, setting to work again with the most determined spirit, and they were cheered on by their partisans to the utmost, and the English goalkeeper had his work cut out to resist the repeated onslaughts of the Northerners. At length their determined play was rewarded with a goal, Renny-Tailyour after a sharp run succeeding in eluding the vigilance of the base-keeper. Once more ends were reversed and play continued until half past four, and although the Scotch men tried all they could to place themselves on an equality with their opponents and several times placed their goal in jeopardy, no other goal resulted, and the representatives of Scotland were again defeated.

40

The status of the international was immediately queried by correspondents to *Bell's Life*, who posed awkward, but pertinent, questions: 'On what grounds do the gentlemen who played on the north country side call themselves representatives of Scotland? Are they recognised in Scotland as representatives of that country?' With the Rugby Football Union having already announced the date for its own 'proper' international against Scotland, the FA's version was starting to look like a pale imitation of the real thing.

However, there were other initiatives for football lovers to enjoy, and two weeks later Sheffield played London for the first time at Bramall Lane. This fixture was important in helping to bring together the codes as played in the two cities, and the initial arrangement was for three matches each season, one in each city according to the home team's rules, and the third with each half of the match played under different rules. This led to confusion for players as well as spectators, who had to remember which code was in force at any given time, and witnessed the bizarre sight of the crossbar being lowered from nine feet to eight feet at half-time.

When Sheffield came south to the Oval in January, due to a 'misunderstanding' they brought an extra man and the game was played 12-a-side. Even so, the match could almost have passed for an England international trial, with London selecting Alcock, Betts, Chenery, Holden, Hooman, Morten, Stephenson, Thompson, Vidal, Welch, Weston and Wollaston. The only one of those who would not play for England at some stage was George Holden of Clapham Rovers, although he came close.[4] The visitors, who travelled down on the Friday in a private railway carriage, were less endowed with internationalists but had the Clegg brothers, Charles and William, in their ranks.

These representative games and the early cup-ties should have made it obvious who would be in contention for places in the second international of the season, but candidates were again asked to write in with nominations.[5] In the event, 20 hopefuls who submitted their names for England were put before the selection panel of club captains. As well as the eventual eleven, they considered Betts, Crake, Holden, Paton, Chappell, Kenrick, Morten, Ruggles-Brise and Benson. Of these, Morten and Chappell had already appeared for Scotland, and it would have made a mockery of the unofficial series if they had been picked for England (although, as it happened, both would be capped for England in full internationals the following season).

41

Scotland had a five-man selection panel of Kirkpatrick, Hogg, Crawford, Lindsay and Kennedy. They were clear who they wanted in their side, but seven first-choice players were not available, including Kirkpatrick and the injured Hogg themselves. Renny-Tailyour had not recovered from a leg knock he picked up playing for Scotland at rugby, and Gladstone was prevented 'by the pressing claims of his official position in connection with the government'. The reasons for the Smith brothers and JN Fulton[6] (of Ravenscourt Park, a rugby club) are less clear, but the cumulative effect was that 'Scotland was most materially weakened by several of their best men not putting in an appearance'.

The FA was acutely conscious of inevitable comparisons with London's first rugby international, organised impeccably at the same venue three weeks earlier. That match, which England won comfortably, attracted around three thousand spectators and the only mishap came at the hands of the photographer, who took a picture of the England team and promptly broke the plate.

It gave rise to much comment on the appeal of rugby to women, who 'enter into the excitement of the match most thoroughly, and many an eye sparkled and many a fair cheek flushed'. In an attempt to broaden the appeal of the football match, the FA provided a tent for ladies (who had to pay extra to gain admission), but only a few took advantage of the facility and *Bell's Life* made the judgement that 'the rugby code is undoubtedly the most popular with the fair sex'.

On 24 February, weather 'of a most cheerless character' put a dampener on the Oval for what proved to be the last of the five unofficial internationals. Although a reasonable crowd turned out, reportedly bigger than previous clashes, it was still under a thousand, and they had to stand around for half an hour as kick-off was delayed while the Scots searched for substitutes.

Of the late recruits, while Henry Stewart was a reasonable choice, being born north of the border, both Charles Thompson (who may have just come along to watch his brother, England's AC Thompson) and Edward Ravenshaw were definitely in the 'emergency' category. It was reported later that Thompson had a vague connection to Scotland as his family owned some property there, but Ravenshaw, a Charterhouse schoolboy, seems to have been roped in at the last minute purely on the pragmatic grounds that he was fit and available.

Montague Muir Mackenzie, who was appointed Scotland captain on his debut in the absence of Kirkpatrick and Hogg, won the toss for choice of positions, but 'for reasons unknown' chose to play into

42

the strong breeze blowing straight down the ground. This made it harder for his makeshift team, who also had to contend with showers that made dribbling difficult as the ground became muddy.

Both teams fielded eight forwards, a half-back, back and goalkeeper, with Muir Mackenzie and Nepean alternating in goal for Scotland, and Stephenson doing the honours for England. All the early pressure was from England, who had several near misses before a mass assault by their forwards created an opening for Clegg to score after about 20 minutes. The change of ends at least gave Scotland some respite from the wind but apart from a couple of ventures upfield it was mainly a case of desperate defending which kept the score down to a single goal.

24 February 1872: unofficial match 5
ENGLAND 1 (Clegg), SCOTLAND 0
Kennington Oval, London

England	*Scotland*
CW Alcock (Wanderers, capt)	MJ Muir Mackenzie (Old Carthusians, capt) *gk 2*
JC Clegg (Sheffield)	HS Ferguson (Royal Artillery)
P Weston (Barnes)	REW Crawford (Harrow Chequers)
RWS Vidal (Westminster)	H Mitchell (Royal Engineers)
AC Thompson (Old Etonians) *h-b*	W Lindsay (Old Wykehamists) *half-back*
E Lubbock (Old Etonians) *back*	CEB Nepean (Oxford Univ) *goalkeeper1*
CW Stephenson (Wanderers) *gk*	FH Crawford (Harrow Chequers)
AG Bonsor (Old Etonians)	EV Ravenshaw (Charterhouse)
TC Hooman (Wanderers)	HH Stewart (Cambridge University)
CHR Wollaston (Oxford Univ)	EHM Elliot (Harrow Chequers) *back*
CJ Chenery (Crystal Palace)	CM Thompson (Trinity College, Cambridge)

Umpire: A Morten (the only official mentioned in reports)

MATCH REPORT
Glasgow Herald

At 25 past three, the game was opened with a kick off from the foot of the English captain. During the first quarter of an hour the advantage was all on the side of the English, as with the wind to help and two of their best backs to support them, their forwards were able to turn their attention to offensive tactics without fear. For some time, however, the defence of Scotland proved equal to the emergency until, at length, a well-sustained rush by the entire body of the English forwards produced a scrimmage in front of the Northern Posts, and a clever kick by Mr JC Clegg settled matters by producing the fall

43

of the Scotch goal, to the intense delight of the English supporters. Exchange of ends followed their achievement, and the Scotch set to work at once, charging and working together with a degree of vigour that seemed to surprise their opponents. So well, indeed, did they utilise their changes that before long the ball was driven right into the very front of the English goal and, but for the great resolution and determined play of its defenders, the fall of that fortress must have inevitably resulted. With this catastrophe averted, the English awoke to the necessity of action, and from this point until the end of the game, the ball rarely left the territory of the Scotch, although there was no lack of energy on the part of the Northern forwards, and Messrs Stewart, RE Crawford and Mitchell all did their utmost to penetrate the lines of defence created by the English backs. On several occasions, Messrs Vidal, Hooman and Weston seriously endangered the safety of the Scotch goal, but the wind and the slippery condition of the ground helped in a great measure to avert its further downfall, and at five minutes to five o'clock, play ceased. To say that the Scots played extremely well is in no way exaggerating, as considering the weak forces at their disposal, and the strength arrayed against them, they may safely be admitted to have shown surprising form. They were certainly the lighter eleven, and this proved to some small extent useful as the slippery state of the ground enabled them to act better than their heavier antagonists. Among their forwards, RE Crawford and Lieutenant Nutshell [sic] dribbled well, and Mr HH Stewart worked hard throughout; while Messrs Lindsay and Elliot, as backs, were most effective. On the side of the victorious eleven, the play was so uniform that selection would be unjust. Perhaps Mr [A] C Thompson was most worthy of notice, as his kicking at half-back was truly brilliant from first to last.

It had been a disappointing contest which did little to dispel the thought that rugby football was in the ascendancy, but at least a flurry of high profile matches, culminating in the first FA Cup final, helped to restore confidence in the association game before the end of the season.

Two days after the third Sheffield v London game, Queen's Park arrived in London to face Wanderers in the FA Cup semi-final, played on Monday 4 March. As a concession to their distant location, they had been granted a bye to this stage of the competition and the match was considered a showdown between the best of England and Scotland. However, the issue was unresolved as it ended without a goal being scored and, with no prospect of returning to London for a replay, Queen's Park were forced to withdraw from the competition.

Rather than heading north immediately, two Queen's Park players, captain Robert Gardner and club secretary David Wotherspoon, stayed on in the capital for the rest of the week and were actually invited to play for Wanderers the following Saturday. In one of football's more unlikely pairings, they were joined in the team against Clapham Rovers by the cricketer, WG Grace, who scored the only goal of the game. (On the same day, Henry Renny-Tailyour and Hugh Mitchell scored the goals which took Royal Engineers into the FA Cup final).

Discussions must have taken place that week about a 'proper' international. The semi-final had demonstrated once and for all that it was quite feasible for a football team to travel the length of the country to play a match, the players taking time off work if necessary. The roaring success of the two rugby internationals, not to mention the London v Sheffield series, only served to press home the point.

Writing to *The Scotsman*[7] the following week, Wotherspoon confirmed that agreement had been reached for Scotland to host an international against England. Aware that rugby was the only football code in Scotland's capital, his letter had a missionary purpose: 'As there may be some players in Edinburgh disposed to take part in it [*i.e.* the international], or at least in the meantime to acquaint themselves with the Association game, may I take the liberty of intimating through your valuable columns that the Queen's Park Club will be happy to afford every opportunity in their power for that purpose. Eleven a side makes an excellent Association game, and the distinctive feature of the play is hands off ball or player.'

The carrot for any interested player was a better chance of beating England, which would be 'a result desirable to all, if it served in any degree to sustain Scottish reputation in manly international competition'. In the event, however, Queen's Park did not play an exhibition match in Edinburgh until December 1873, and even then Association rules were so little known in the east that they had to bring their own goalposts with them from Glasgow.[8]

By the time Wotherspoon's letter was published, Wanderers had won the first FA Cup, defeating Royal Engineers 1-0 with a team full of England players. Association football was now firmly established, and the scene was set for its full international debut.

---

[1] The FA Cup was organised by a five man committee: CW Alcock, J Kirkpatrick, RH Birkett, A Stair and J Powell.

[2] According to *The Scotsman*: 'Crawford, owing to the long journey from Edinburgh, hardly showed his best form.'

[3] Alfred Stair (1845-1914) of Upton Park, who refereed the first three FA Cup finals.

[4] Holden, who had learned his football at Brentwood School, played for the South v North in 1870, and for London v Sheffield and Nottingham. He was a named reserve for England in November 1872 and would surely have played had he not been ill.

[5] *Bell's Life*, 10 February 1872.

[6] John Napier Fulton, born 1848 in Glasgow, was a lawyer in London. He was killed in the *Lusitania* disaster of 1915.

[7] *The Scotsman*, 18 March 1872.

[8] The match in 1873 was notably successful as it captured the imagination of many of Edinburgh's young sportsmen and was the catalyst for numerous clubs being formed.

Chapter 5

THE REAL THING AT LAST

1872: the world's first association football international

SOFT FALLING, FORTUNATELY

MARION WOTHERSPOON'S nimble fingers were hard at work. Her younger brother David was in the Scotland team to face England, and she wanted to be sure the players looked their best, embroidering a red lion rampant on the eleven blue shirts.

Her handiwork was so impressive that the badge was adopted by the Scotland national team and is still worn by them today. Unfortunately, if pictures of the match are accurate, the lions were sewn on back to front.[1]

It was clear by 1872 that continuing to limit the England and Scotland teams to those who lived in and around London was unsustainable if the FA was to make headway in its mission to take association football to a wider public. While much of the focus in that respect was on the Scotland eleven, it should not be forgotten that England was also largely a London side, and had ignored players from Nottingham and Sheffield (Charles Clegg being the exception, and only in the last of the five).

The rugby football fraternity had shown the way with the first Scotland v England match in Edinburgh in 1871, and the return in London a year later. Further evidence of the feasibility of travelling four hundred miles to play football was established by Queen's Park taking part in the initial FA Cup competition.

There was still no national organisation in Scotland – the Scottish FA would not be established until March 1873, two weeks after the Scottish Rugby Union – but the Queen's Park committee members were sufficiently emboldened by their draw with Wanderers, an England v Scotland encounter in all but name, to take up the challenge. They agreed to host the first international match in Glasgow and took on responsibility for all the arrangements and for selecting the Scotland team.

Initially, they opened the net wide for players and the build-up to the first 'true' association football international began in October when Archibald Rae, secretary of Queen's Park, appealed for recruits in the press: 'Will you allow me, through your columns, to invite Scotch players who may wish to take part in this match to send their names and addresses to me, either direct, or through their captain or secretary, no later than Monday 21st, so as to allow time for co-operation and practice.'[2]

There were numerous applicants, and the club hosted a practice match on 9 November but it was ruined by heavy rain, the ground being 'chiefly marsh and pond' and 'the quantity of mud carried off by the players at the end of the game was tremendous'.[3] Even so, it was useful in identifying potential players and particular praise was given to the rugby international Thomas Chalmers of Glasgow Academicals, who was 'a capital goalkeeper, albeit the rules were new to him'. Chalmers was duly included in a squad of 17 possible players, alongside two more rugby caps, William Cross and Henry Renny-Tailyour. Arthur Kinnaird was given his place as 'captain of the London-Scotch international team,' and there was a mention for the Rev James Barclay of Dumfries. The other 12 were all Queen's Park members.

A second trial was played at Burnbank, the home of Glasgow Academicals, on the afternoon of Wednesday 20 November but, again, wet ground conspired against good football and several players failed to put in an appearance. Three days later, Chalmers and Cross played at the same venue in the first Glasgow v Edinburgh rugby match; it was still raining, and Edinburgh added to the home side's gloom by winning.

As Queen's Park had no ground of their own, playing on open recreation ground, the club needed to find a suitable venue to stage the international. Burnbank had been offered free of charge by the Academical club, but it was not enclosed and the Queen's Park committee decided instead to take the game to Hamilton Crescent in Partick, the home of West of Scotland Cricket Club, even if it meant paying a fee. Hamilton Crescent had echoes of Kennington Oval in that it was an established sports ground, home to West of Scotland since 1862 not just for cricket but also in regular use for rugby matches through the winter and for athletics. It was probably the biggest enclosed space for sport in Glasgow at that time, could not be entered without payment, and provided ample spectator accommodation. It is still in use today, with only a slight encroachment of housing on its southern edge to change the original layout.

The football pitch was laid out north-south from the pavilion towards Partick Burgh Hall, and although it had a pronounced slope, it was preferable to the surface at Burnbank which was condemned after the trial by the *Glasgow Herald* as 'very sloppy; little ponds here and there agreeably relieving the otherwise dreary landscape'. The wise choice of Partick was echoed three months later when the same ground hosted the rugby international.

By this time, it appears that voices within Queen's Park argued that, as their club had taken on the entire responsibility of arranging the match, its reputation was at stake; therefore, the honour of representing Scotland should be restricted to its members. When the home team was announced on 25 November, there was no place for any of the outsiders who had featured in the 'possible' selection: all eleven players were members of Queen's Park, and so were the two reserves, William Keay and Alexander Broadfoot.

As if to emphasise the point, the Scotland team would play in blue jerseys, white knickerbockers, and blue and white striped stockings; which just happened to be the Queen's Park colours of the time. The only embellishments were Marion Wotherspoon's lion rampant badges.

Kinnaird and Renny-Tailyour were not asked to travel north but would at least be called upon in the return match in the spring,

49

while the rugby players and the Reverend Barclay were never given a second chance.[4]

Determination in goal from Scotland captain Robert Gardner

Robert Gardner, captain of Queen's Park, was naturally appointed to the same role for Scotland, although his son Bob later recalled that the responsibility did not weigh too heavily on his shoulders: 'He certainly was a very serious-minded man, but he looked upon football as nothing more than healthy exercise, the means to giving expression to sportsmanship. He told me afterwards that while he was keenly desirous of Scotland winning, there must be no loss of sleep over the thought of defeat. It was to be a meeting between two teams of sportsmen with a love of football, with no thought of rancour whatever the result.'[5]

The FA was also busy, their need for a trial effectively met by London's trip to Sheffield on 2 November. The cities had met three times the previous season, and the fixture had quickly grown sufficiently in stature to attract an 'immense assemblage' of 5,000 spectators at Bramall Lane. Because of the continuing differences in rules, the London side struggled to adapt to the Sheffield rules and lost 4-1, with the offside rule said to be 'so diametrically opposed to the usages of the south as to be unpalatable to the southerners generally'.[6]

The FA committee met on Thursday 14 November, when they not only selected an eleven but also decided that the team would wear white jerseys with the England arms embroidered on left breast, dark blue caps, and white flannel trousers or knickerbockers. Remarkably, one of the shirts, that worn by AK Smith, has survived and is now in the National Football Museum.

Their original selection was Alcock (Wanderers), Betts (Harrow Chequers), Chenery (Crystal Palace), Clegg (Sheffield), Greenhalgh (Nottingham), Morten (Crystal Palace), F McLean (a pseudonym for Frederick Chappell), Morice (Barnes), Ottaway (Oxford University), Hooman (Wanderers) and Welch (Wanderers). When the team was provided to *The Scotsman*, Victorian humour changed the name of Morten to Lesten, while TC Hooman was given as CT Whichman. Two reserves were named, Holden (Clapham Rovers) and Maynard (1st Surrey Rifles), and the other candidates were Brockbank (Cambridge University), Barker (Hertfordshire Rangers), HB Soden (Crystal Palace) and AB Baillon (Nottingham).

Alcock, England's captain in all five unofficial internationals, fully expected to lead out the team for their first cross-border match but his plans were thrown into painful disarray on 16 November, when his reputation for vigorous play caught up with him. A friendly between the old boys of Eton and Harrow, described as 'a friendly, but most vicious game of football'[7] ended with Alcock so badly hurt that it not only put him out of this game, it also set in train a series of injuries that blighted his international career. When he attempted a comeback in the spring he broke down and missed the return match; not until 1875 would he play for England, and then only once.

This ticket to the first international is now on display in the Scottish Football Museum

As well as Alcock being disabled, Betts was in 'a similar state', Hooman and Holden were ill, and Morten was prevented from playing for unspecified reasons. Brockbank, Barker and Maynard were drafted in from the original list of candidates, and the final place went to Sheffield's AK Smith, now in his final year of study at Oxford University. Hardly surprising, then, that *The Scotsman* on 27 November reported gleefully 'things are not favouring the Englishmen in their preparations ... indeed everything is going wrong'.

The match was well promoted, with tickets on sale and newspaper adverts in the days before the match, which pointed out that extra buses would go on direct to the ground from the foot of Miller Street in Glasgow city centre. There were even fears that the ground would not be able to cope with the anticipated large crowd, and a letter to the *Glasgow Herald* suggested that admission should be by ticket only. An anxious response on the day of the game pointed out how unfair this would be: 'I do not know the committee of management, nor anyone who has tickets to dispose of, and it would be too bad if I had my journey to Partick for nothing.' In the event, the crowd behaved impeccably: 'The ground was roped and staked, and though here and there the stakes were not equal to the strain upon them, the onlookers kept perfect order, and never once trenched upon the field of play. Indeed, we have never seen a match where order was so well observed, with so little appearance of keeping it.'[8]

The spectators had to be relatively affluent to be able to afford the shilling entry fee, for which they stood behind ropes strung between wooden stakes along the touchlines.

Admission cost a shilling, with or without ticket, and although many accounts refer to 4,000 spectators, some contemporary newspapers put the figure at around 2,500. The latter is more realistic in the light of gate receipts that were sixpence short of £103, equating to just over two thousand admissions at a shilling each (ladies were admitted free). Out of this, Queen's Park had to pay the match costs, including £20 to West of Scotland CC for use of their ground, and footed the bill for dinner that evening, all of which totalled £69 11s 6d. Overall the international generated a surplus of £33 and 8 shillings – not bad for a club which had less than £8 in the bank at the start of the season – and this profit was set aside as a travel fund for the return match.

Kick-off was about 15 minutes later than the advertised time of 2pm, after the two teams made final preparations on the pitch, as observed in some style by William Ralston[9] in *The Graphic*, a weekly pictorial. His series of nine drawings capture beautifully the mood of the event: the English players warming up while smoking pipes or cheroots, the wild-eyed determination of Gardner in goal, Mackinnon's sensational overhead kick, the charging and shoving that was all part of the game, the top-hatted crowd straining the ropes. Ralston's drawings are the only images of the match; a photographer had been commissioned, but sadly he packed up and left when the Scotland players refused to commit to purchasing his prints.

William Ralston depicted the players warming up while smoking pipes and cheroots

There were marked physical discrepancies between the teams, as the *Glasgow Herald* observed: 'The Englishmen had all the advantage of weight, their average being about two stones heavier than the Scotchmen and they had also the advantage in pace. The strong point of the home club [*sic*] was that they played excellently well together.' This allusion to the combination play of the Scots highlighted the differing playing styles, with Queen's Park promoting a passing game that was alien to the English, who had been brought up on a diet of individual dribbling and 'backing up', which required a strong physical presence.

It was perhaps a legacy of the need for the Englishmen to adapt to association rules after their diverse school football experiences; their tendency to play as individuals upset Charles Clegg, who later confessed to remembering very little about the match except that his team mates played for themselves, coming to the conclusion that some of them were awful snobs and not much troubled about a 'mon fra' Sheffield'.[10] The Scots had no such inhibitions, however, and the Queen's Park members had long understood that teamwork was the most effective way of playing the game.

William Mackinnon's overhead kick was one of the highlights of the match, his athletic clearance taking the English by surprise

Both sides were proficient in their own way, and the detailed match report indicates a thrilling end-to-end struggle between two well-matched sides. Chances were few, and Scotland came closest to scoring on the stroke of half time, as a shot from Leckie struck the tape across the top of the goal and bounded over, while Ottaway had a shot which was saved. There was the quirk of both sides changing their goalkeeper at half-time, with Barker trading places with Maynard, and Gardner did likewise with Robert Smith although he returned between the posts during the second half.

After ninety minutes of energetic play, the game ended in stalemate. It would be almost a hundred years before the next goal-less game between the nations, but this did not seem to matter at the time and a draw was accepted as a fair result.

The teams had dinner together in the city centre at Carrick's Royal Hotel in George Square, toasting the health of the game in all its guises, even the Sheffield FA and the Scotland rugby team.

They played a return towards the end of the season, Scotland travelling to London in March 1873 for a match at the Oval which England won 4-2. A week after that, the Scottish Football Association was formed. The rest, as they say, is history.

30 November 1872
SCOTLAND 0, ENGLAND 0
West of Scotland Cricket Ground, Glasgow

Scotland
R Gardner (Queen's Park, capt) *goalkeeper, then forward*
W Ker (Granville and Queen's Park) *back*
J Taylor (Queen's Park) *back*
JJ Thomson (Queen's Park) *half-back*
J Smith (South Norwood and Queen's Park) *half-back*
R Smith (South Norwood and Queen's Park) *forward, then goalkeeper*
JB Weir (Queen's Park) *forward*
R Leckie (Queen's Park) *forward*
A Rhind (Queen's Park) *forward*
WM Mackinnon (Queen's Park) *forward*
D Wotherspoon (Queen's Park) *forward*

England
R Barker (Hertfordshire Rangers) *goalkeeper, then forward*
EH Greenhalgh (Notts Club) *back*
RC Welch (Harrow Chequers and Wanderers) *half-back*
F Chappell (Oxford University) *'fly kick'*
CJ Ottaway (Oxford University, capt) *forward*
AK Smith (Oxford University) *forward*
CJ Chenery (Crystal Palace) *forward*
JC Clegg (Sheffield) *forward*
J Brockbank (Cambridge University) *forward*
WJ Maynard (1st Surrey Rifles) *forward, then goalkeeper*
CJ Morice (Barnes) *forward*

Umpires: CW Alcock (Hon Secretary of the FA)
and HN Smith[11] (President of Queen's Park).
Referee: W Keay (Hon Treasurer, Queen's Park).

HARD STRUGGLE—

MATCH REPORT[12]
Glasgow Evening News

Close upon two o'clock both teams appeared on the field with the punt-about. The Englishmen were much superior in weight to their more diminutive, but wiry and active opponents. Scotland having won the toss, elected to play downhill. England kicked off at a quarter past two o'clock. Scotland, playing well together, at once carried the ball well on their opponents' goal, but the Southron backs were all there, and sent the leather flying up among their forwards, who, by a combined rush, to the half up the hill, and for a few minutes closely besieged the home goal – one or two long shies not quite making their mark. The ball being shortly after kicked behind gave Scotland the corner kick-off, which they used well, running the ball again well down the hill, only to be turned however by the ever-watchful Welch.

Runs for both sides in turn now became the order of the day, Ottaway and Kirke Smith dribbling beautifully for England, and Weir and Leckie playing well up for Scotland. After a good 'crowd up' for England, the ball was 'handed' by Thomson, which gave England a free kick, but though only about twenty yards from goal nothing was made of it. Weir here got on the ball again, and sided it rapidly down the hill, but the slope made him lose his command of the ball, and Welch again sent it north of the Tweed, and Morice and Maynard getting it, backing up well, and closely followed by their middles made things lively for Scotland, but the back play of Ker and Taylor was too much for the attack, and relieved the goal from danger. Even play for a little, with not a little charging, R Smith doing his full share of this, till Brockbank got the ball at his toe, and exhibited a splendid piece of dribbling, passing half a dozen of his opponents, but making little of his work, having dribbled almost across the field instead of towards the Scotch goal. Another foul close on the Scotch goal, this time by Wotherspoon, gave England another free kick, which brought the ball so close on goal that with their great weight forward, made the prospect serious; but Thomson and Taylor 'hindering' well, Ker came to the rescue, and by a splendid kick from among quite a crowd of his opponents, opened the lungs of Scottish onlookers.

From the throw in the ball was taken off by Rhind, who, with Mackinnon and R Smith playing well together, brought the tears to Southern eyes, but Greenhalgh and Barker dried them. This gave the ball to Clegg, who made a short run, but was neatly turned. Both sides were working very hard, and showing excellent play. Brockbank and Clegg were off again, the former dribbling very neatly and effectively; both well backed up by the middles, seemed likely to carry everything before them; but Ker was there, and he refused to let them carry the ball – a splendid kick of his sending the ball well into England's quarters. The kick was well followed by Scotland – Mackinnon cleverly dodging Clegg and Chappell, and middling the ball. Welch was there as usual, however, and as he thought neutral territory was the proper place for the ball, he sent it there. Kirke Smith thought it ought to be nearer the Scotch goal. He started with it, dodged ably past several opponents, but found Thomson too quick for him.

Weir then took charge of the ball and carried it in fine style past both forwards and backs, and seemed likely to score, but England kicked the ball into touch. England got the throw in, and their middles, conspicuously Kirke Smith and Ottaway, took the ball to the middle of the field again, where some delightful play took place, several men on both sides showing well. Mackinnon got the ball out and clearly backed by Rhind, dodged his opponents till well on the English goal, but alas for the vanity of human wishes, Barker put the ball well up the field. Here Maynard and Morice got hold of it, and made a good rush, which was effectively brought to an untimely end by Taylor, who went to grass in the process. But the ball was sent back, and was soon well up the hill, the Scotch goal-keeper getting his kick spoiled, which put the goal in jeopardy; but of course Ker was there, and kicked the ball out well down the touch line. The 'flying ball' it is truly, for it was soon across the field, where Rhind got behind it, and dribbled it rapidly down the field. Greenhalgh, however, didn't seem to want the ball there, so he sent it up again. But it soon came back. Wotherspoon, R Smith and Weir, *playing well together, got the leather down on the English goal, and kept blood at fever heat there for a little. But Barker got it out. Not far enough, though; for Leckie, after a very short dribble, took a shot at goal, which roused the enthusiastic shouts of the spectators, who thought the ball had gone under. Alas, no! It struck the tape, but unfortunately, instead of going under, it rolled over. A close shave; but shaves don't count. Just as the umpires gave this 'no goal' time was called, and was changed.*

For England, Barker (goal) and Maynard (forward) changed places, while Gardner (goal) and R Smith (forward) changed places for Scotland. England now had the hill. Wotherspoon took a good kick off, which the English back failed to return. In a trice Rhind had passed, and got on the ball, but kicked it into touch. The throw in was close on the goal line, giving Scotland a chance for goal, which England would not allow them to utilise. Shortly after they had another shot at goal, but the ball was skied, and went well over the tape.

The kick-off was England's, and gave Clegg a chance, which he accepted, running the ball well into the Scotch quarters, and now began the most exciting bit of play of a remarkably well contested match. Clegg was stopped by J Smith, who pushed the ball forward to Wotherspoon. The latter started with it, playing the ball beautifully, but was stopped by Greenhalgh, who gave the ball to his own forwards. Ottaway got on it, dribbled it with admirable skill close on the Scottish goal, and took a straight shot, which R Smith smartly stopped, and got away. But it was back at goal again immediately and a severe tussle took place, just at the side of goal, the ball being again and again kicked and stopped, till finally it was got behind and Scotland breathed again. R Smith was sent forward, and Gardner resumed his place at goal. Both sides were striving hard to score. No effort was spared, and brilliant play – play in every respect worthy of an international contest – was shown by both teams.

The English mettled up keenly and pressed Scotland hard, but the home back play was superb and equal to every emergency, Ker especially never failing to lift the ball and kicking wonderfully. Of the forwards at this time Ottaway and Kirke Smith were prominent for England, and Weir, R Smith and Rhind for Scotland. Mackinnon, who is not tall, here made a very clever kick. The ball was on the bound higher than his head, when he leaped up and to the surprise of his opponent, who was waiting till the ball came over Mackinnon, kicked it well up the hill. The kick was much admired, and lustily applauded.

Shortly after England had the throw in near the home goal-line, and a hard struggle followed in the effort of the Southrons to put the ball under the tape, during which a few on both sides went to grass, but R Smith got the ball, and cleverly ran the goal free. 'Turn about' for a little, and Scotland was again pressed – now close on the call of time – both sides fighting hard. Brockbank and Chenery got the ball sided down on the Scotch goal-line, but

58

Ker turned it, and leaving his own post, closed the match by the most brilliant run of the day, dribbling the ball past the whole field close upon the English lines before he was stopped, time being called just as England turned the ball. Thus a most exciting and satisfactory match ended in a draw, neither side having gained anything, and the play throughout having been very even.

---

[1] Marion Wotherspoon was also prevailed upon in succeeding years: the SFA accounts for 1874 reveal that David Wotherspoon was paid 12 shillings for six 'lions' for the international team, equating to the six newly-capped players that year, and presumably he was gentleman enough to pass the money on to his sister.

[2] *Glasgow Herald*, 15 October 1872, and *The Scotsman*, 19 October 1872.

[3] *Glasgow Herald*, 11 November 1872

[4] Not all accounts agree with this. Some reports state that Kinnaird and Renny-Tailyour were 'not available', and that Chalmers excluded himself on the grounds of unfamiliarity with association rules.

[5] Quoted by WG Gallagher in *Association Football* (1960), Vol. iv, p8. However, Robert Gardner junior was only 13 when his father died, so these reflections may not be entirely accurate.

[6] *Penny Illustrated Paper*, 9 November 1872

[7] *The Graphic*, 23 November 1872

[8] *Glasgow Evening News*, 2 December 1872

[9] Ralston went on to a successful career as an illustrator with *Punch* and also ran a photography studio in Glasgow.

[10] JAH Catton, *Wickets and Goals*, p171

[11] Henry Norris Smith (1831/2-1892)

[12] This match report was found among the papers of Scotland forward William Ker; although unmarked, it appears to come from the *Glasgow Evening News*, 2 December 1872.

Chapter 6

'GONE TO THE ROCKY MOUNTAINS'

Pioneer stories

The influence of the early international players went around the world, as this was the age of Empire. Many of them made their careers abroad when their playing days were over; some were successful, a few died far from home, and they all had stories to tell.

'HE IS a squint-eyed, consumptive liar, with breath like a buzzard and a record like a convict.' Ouch! Robert Smith may have had tough opponents in his football days, but nothing compared to this stream of invective from a rival newspaper editor in Wyoming.

What was a former Scottish football internationalist doing in the American West? Quite simply, Smith was an adventurer all his life: he was a founding member of Scotland's first association football club, he was the first man to play association football on both sides of the border, took part in the inaugural FA Cup competition, and represented his country. Then, having made his mark, he disappeared from view. All the early football annuals could say about him was: 'gone to the Rocky Mountains'. Little did they know this Scottish pioneer was continuing to make waves on the other side of the Atlantic.

Smith was born in Aberdeen in 1848, third son of the Earl of Fife's gardener, who was then based at Mar Lodge on Deeside. When his father became head gardener at Innes House, the Earl's estate near Elgin, Robert entered Fordyce Academy, a privately endowed school with a high reputation. In four years there he not only received a sound education, he became close friends with William Klingner, the son of a German doctor[1] based in the Morayshire fishing village of Portsoy.

When Smith left school in 1864, he went to Glasgow to work for the publisher William Mackenzie[2], and was joined in the city by Klingner. Being country boys they liked to get plenty of fresh air and took to exercising on open ground on the south side of the city with

60

other young men, many with similar origins in the north of Scotland. They started kicking a ball about and in the summer of 1867 founded Queen's Park FC; Klingner was appointed secretary, with Smith on the committee. Football was not Robert's only passion, and he won silver cups at the prestigious West of Scotland Cricket Club athletic sports in 1869, winning the steeplechase and long jump.

Smith was by then working as a cashier for shipping insurance brokers Hutchison & Brown but in 1869 his employers went out of business, so he had to find a new job, and ended up in London in a similar role for Sir Charles Price & Co, oil merchants; he shared digs in the capital with Klingner. He continued in football with South Norwood but retained close links to Queen's Park, who nominated him in 1870 to play for Scotland in the second unofficial international, and he turned out for the club when they came to London in the 1872 FA Cup semi-final against Wanderers. They also nominated him for the FA committee, where he effectively represented Scottish football.

Meanwhile, his older brother James had joined him in London in 1871, working as a commercial representative for an artists' suppliers, and he too played for South Norwood. Both brothers were capped for Scotland in the first football international in November 1872, and Robert was also selected for the return in the spring. He was an industrious player without being particularly gifted, according to one observer: 'while no man ever worked harder in the field, or did more for a club, he was not what could be called a brilliant forward.'[3]

Soon, he was on the move again. Intrigued by the potential of America, in 1873 he accepted the position of cashier with the Rocky Mountain Coal and Iron Co in Wyoming. In difficult conditions – the township of Almy where he lived was little more than a tented camp – he lasted three years, then briefly tried his hand at silver mining over the border in Utah, returning to Wyoming in the latter part of 1877.

By then, his brother was dead. James had taken over Robert's role on the FA committee, and continued to play for South Norwood. However, after his last game in January 1876 he fell ill, returned home to his parents in Moray, and died there in the autumn of a stroke.

Robert settled in the town of Green River, where he opened a grocery store in partnership with his old friend William Klingner, selling everything from oysters to lumber. He also took up politics, and was elected a member of the Wyoming House of Representatives. Sufficiently established, he travelled to Glasgow to marry in 1879, bringing his new wife Georgina back with him. His former colleagues from Queen's Park presented him with a testimonial, but that was the last time they saw him.

The first advert for the store opened in 1878 by Robert Smith and William Klingner, two founders of Queen's Park FC who were making new lives in Wyoming

He was clearly a busy man, and as well as starting a family he launched the county's first newspaper, the weekly *Sweetwater Gazette*. It soon became a power in local and state politics, although Smith's views upset Bill Nye, a notoriously cantankerous editor of the rival *Laramie Boomerang*, who wrote: 'We have nothing more to say of the editor of the *Sweetwater Gazette*. Aside from the fact that he is a squint-eyed, consumptive liar, with a breath like a buzzard and a record like a convict, we don't know anything against him. He means well enough, and if he can evade the penitentiary and the vigilance committee for a few more years, there is a chance for him to end his life in a natural way. If he don't tell the truth a little more plenty, however, the Green River people will rise as one man and churn him up till there won't be anything left of him but a pair of suspenders and a wart.'[4]

Smith just laughed it off, and the turn of phrase amused so many people that it was repeated in other newspapers and even published in a book of Bill Nye's collective writing.

As a throwback to his sporting days, Smith tried to establish football locally and put together a Green River eleven to challenge Rock Springs. Played on 4 July 1883, the game attracted 300 spectators who saw his side lose 4-0, 'in spite of the violent exertions of their captain'. Soccer never did catch on in Wyoming in his lifetime.

Smith became frustrated by the lack of civic progress being made by Green River, and in 1887 published in his newspaper a list of all the things the town was lacking: a dentist, a bank, a harness shop, a photographer, a larger schoolhouse, more sidewalks and better ones, a library, a gymnasium, a good church choir and 'a thoroughly organised emigration society that will induce men of money and energy to locate in our midst'.

He was not prepared to hang around waiting for all this to happen, and promptly relocated 15 miles east to Rock Springs, taking his printing press with him. He renamed his newspaper the *Rock Springs Miner* and it went from strength to strength; in fact, it is still going, as the *Rocket-Miner*. An ardent Republican, he used the paper (successfully) to further his political ambitions: 'His editorials have now wide publicity, while upon all matters of controversy he is considered a formidable though courteous antagonist, never stooping to personal attacks nor resorting to anything savoring of undignified journalism.'

Looking magnificent in Highland dress, Robert Smith (centre) was Chief of the Rock Springs Caledonian Club *(courtesy of Bobbi Smith)*

He played an integral part in local society, became Chief of the Rock Springs Caledonian Club, and won praise for his contribution to the development of Sweetwater County: 'He has been an earnest worker for every enterprise that tends to the development of the social, educational and moral interests of the city and county and every measure having the public welfare for its object finds in him a zealous supporter and liberal patron. Being a well-educated man, he has been especially interested in the matter of schools, realizing that intelligence generally diffused, is one of the state's most important safeguards.'[5]

Robert Smith in his Oklahoma office, where he ran a business selling mineral leasing rights in the former Creek and Cherokee nations *(courtesy of Bobbi Smith)*

In 1888 he was elected to represent Sweetwater in the Territorial Council of Wyoming (statehood was still two years away), which meant frequent railroad trips to Cheyenne but gave him the title, the Honorable Robert Smith. Although he served just one term on the Council, he remained involved in politics and was appointed in 1902 as chief clerk of the House of Representatives in the Seventh State Legislature. Many people were surprised when Smith decided in 1903 to sell his newspaper and take a job in Indian Territory (which formed part of the new state of Oklahoma a few years later). He was appointed head of the lease department in the former Creek and Cherokee nations, which had been set up ostensibly to help Native Americans to sell the oil and gas exploitation rights for their land. Within two years he resigned from the post to set up his own business, as he realised the potential profits he could make in selling these leases himself.

Robert Smith was buried in Chicago, with a thistle on his gravestone to honour his Scottish roots (*courtesy of Graceland Cemetery*)

He remained in the town of Muskogee with his wife until his retirement, while his daughter remained close, marrying an Oklahoma lawyer, and his son became a doctor in Chicago. In 1914, his health in decline, Smith travelled to see his son for medical treatment, but after undergoing an operation he failed to recover and died in the windy city.

A most gentlemanly young fellow

International footballers are not usually associated with key scientific advances yet William Ker, while no scientist himself, was closely linked to the development of the telephone and television. He married into the extended family of Alexander Graham Bell, inventor of the telephone, and duly found himself working on the introduction of the new instrument to the UK; his father, meanwhile, undertook ground-breaking research into the properties of light that would be a key element in the creation of early television sets.

William was the second son of Scottish physicist John Kerr[6], but he and his brothers amended their surnames to become Ker, on the insistence of their mother. William explained: 'My father spelled the name with two rs, but we three boys all spell it with one, as my mother said it should be spelled. Although my father always stuck to the way his father spelled the name he let my mother have her way with the family. We were all Kers at school from my earliest recollection.'[7]

65

William Ker as a young man
(courtesy of Graham Johnson)

Ker started work in a Glasgow bank while still living with his parents in Mount Florida, on the south side of the city. He was in the right place at the right time to become involved in the early development of football, joining two clubs which played nearby, Granville (based at Myrtle Park) and Queen's Park, who were still using the local recreation ground. Although often listed as captain of Granville in reports of the first international, his fame arose from his membership of the latter. He travelled to London for the semi-final of the first FA Cup competition in 1872; the match against Wanderers ended 0-0, and as Queen's Park could not afford to return for a replay, they scratched from the competition. The following season, Ker played in the first two internationals for Scotland against England. He was a fine leader, according to DD Bone: 'William Ker did much by his tact and ability to bring on our senior club to seek new conquests in England. Mr Ker was a most gentlemanly young fellow, and made himself respected by club companions and opponents alike.'[8]

A dedicated committee member as well as a good footballer, he was allocated the role of writing to potential patrons for the club, including the Prince of Wales (who turned it down), was elected honorary treasurer of the newly founded Scottish Football Association in March 1873, then made club captain that summer. When Queen's Park decided to build an enclosed ground Ker was heavily involved in the search for a suitable arena, and played in the game which opened the first Hampden Park in October 1873, thereby becoming one of the few men to play in both the FA Cup and Scottish Cup. In this match, a 7-0 victory over Dumbreck, Queen's Park wore black and white hoops for the first time; previously they had dark blue shirts, which were adopted as the Scotland national team colours.

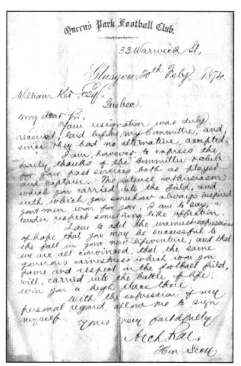

Queen's Park secretary Archibald Rae sent this appreciative letter to William Ker when he resigned from the club to emigrate to Canada (*courtesy of Graham Johnson*)

A month later he resigned from the club, having decided to emigrate. Ker arrived first in Ontario, finding work in the Imperial Bank of Canada alongside a young man called Charles Bell. Their friendship would have a marked influence on his future direction, not least when, in 1876, he married Charles's sister Lily.[9] The Bells were cousins of Alexander Graham Bell, who was living nearby and conducting the experiments that would lead to his patent of the first telephone in 1876. The new invention soon spread to other countries, and when Charles was appointed general manager of the National Telephone Company in 1879, he asked William to come back with him to Britain to help with the launch. For a year and a half, William and his wife (they had three sons by then) lived in Leeds, as he managed the opening of the first telephone exchanges in Yorkshire and the north.

He decided in late 1881 to return to America, continuing in the same line of business as general manager of the Pennsylvania Telephone Company. Five successful years later, the board of directors formally minuted 'that in accepting the resignation of our general manager, this company cannot but express its hearty endorsement of him as a man and as a most intelligent officer, and our sincere regret at the loss of his most valuable service.'

His next move was much further west, in the Yakima Valley, Washington State, where he arrived in 1886 to establish a 7,000 acre farm at Moxee. Keeping the enterprise in the family, the other founders of the Moxee Company included Charles Bell and Gardiner Greene Hubbard (whose daughter Mabel had married Alexander Graham Bell). The Moxee venture was, in many respects, experimental and depended on introducing irrigation to the arid soil with the construction of a canal. Tobacco was grown, and the company's factory produced its own brand of cigars, but not with commercial success. Far more appropriate to the soil were hops, and today about two thirds of the hops grown in the USA originate in Yakima County. The other aim of the farm was to sell parcels of newly-irrigated land to incoming settlers.

William and Lily Ker later in life
(courtesy of Graham Johnson)

William was general manager of Moxee only until 1891, when he handed over to his younger brother George, another talented footballer who won the Scottish Cup three times with Queen's Park and notched ten goals in five appearances for Scotland, including a hat-trick against England on his debut in 1880. George achieved all this before giving up the game aged 22 to emigrate to America, first learning cattle herding skills at a ranch in Texas, then travelling to join the venture at Moxee, where he settled for the rest of his life.[10]

William moved east to Washington DC to become a real estate broker until his retirement. He had not forgotten his playing days, however, and wrote to his daughter a few months before his death in 1925: 'I suffered a good deal from my old football shins, which I knocked several times chopping wood.' He is buried in the city's Rock Creek cemetery.

Lonely graves

Not all travelling footballers were fortunate enough to prosper and some of them ended up dying in obscure places, far from home.

When it comes to the most remote regions on earth, the Australian outback is right up with the best of them. That was the sad fate of Scotland international James Biggar Weir, who succumbed to illness in a distant railway construction camp. It took three weeks for the news even to reach his wife.

It was a sad end for the man once known as the Prince of Dribblers. Weir had a rare talent for ball control, valued even in a passing team like Queen's Park, and one opponent ascribed his dribbling to the fact that his bandy legs formed a 'crab-like' circle from which the ball could not escape.

DD Bone wrote affectionately: 'Who could dribble and keep possession of the ball like Weir? In a football sense he was in everybody's mouth sixteen years ago, when crack forwards were few, and neat dribblers fewer. In all the contests the Queen's Park engaged in for ten years, none was more popular among the spectators, and emulated by the then young generation of players, than Weir. Well can I remember the match at Hampden Park against the London Wanderers when Weir, being tackled by the Hon AF Kinnaird and CW Alcock, put his foot on the ball, shook off the two powerful Englishmen, and made a goal.'[11]

Weir, who won four caps for Scotland and three Scottish Cups, was the youngest son of a Glasgow house builder, William Weir, whose business prospered during the rapid expansion of the city's south side. Brought up in Langside, the young man worked as a joiner for the family business while playing for Queen's Park throughout the 1870s, but after his father's death in 1880, rather than work for his older brother, he decided to emigrate to Australia.

He arrived in Adelaide on the Orient Line steamship SS *John Elder* in mid-October 1881, after a six week journey. In South Australia he evidently married and towards the end of the decade found work on the ambitious project to build a transcontinental railway all the way from the south coast to Darwin in the north. Early in 1889 he was based at Warrina, about 620 miles north of Adelaide, where a largely tented and temporary community had been set up in a dusty creek bed. With a few hundred workers and other residents, for two years it was the Head Camp for work on the Great Northern Extension Railway, popularly known as the *Ghan* after the Afghan camel drivers who helped to open up the route.

Conditions were harsh, and when Weir fell ill he was cared for in the primitive Warrina hospital, which did not have the means to treat his typhoid fever and congestion of the lungs. He fought for over three weeks before succumbing on 23 April.

Word did not reach his (unnamed) wife for three weeks, and it was not until 13 May that she inserted a death announcement in the *Adelaide Advertiser*. She spelled his middle name wrongly as Biger rather than Biggar, and despite adding 'Glasgow papers copy' the notice did not reach Scotland. It was months before word filtered home that the great player had died, and he was never properly commemorated in his homeland. Meanwhile, somewhere in the outback, one of Scotland's finest pioneers lies in an unmarked grave.

Another Scottish pioneer to end up in a remote part of Australia was George Croughly Gordon, who played in the first unofficial international. Born in London to a Scots family – his middle name Croughly comes from the ancestral farm near Tomintoul, Banffshire – Gordon went to school at Clapham Grammar School, so it is little surprise that he ended up playing for CCC, the football team of Clapham Cricket Club. However, he could not be considered a first rank player and his sole appearance for Scotland was as a late substitute. His main sport was, in fact, rowing and he won a number of prizes, most notably the Grand Challenge Cup in 1876 with Thames RC.

He spent ten years with the Civil Service as a clerk in the Queen's Bench Office, before deciding to emigrate to New Zealand. There, he went into partnership at Auckland with his former school friend Charles Craven Dacre (who had played football for Surrey and Kent v Middlesex in 1867). Their merchant enterprise was a useful start to life in the colony but did not last long, and in February 1881 he established a partnership with CJ Hutchinson, selling grain.

When this, too, was dissolved the following year, Gordon crossed over to Australia where he set up another company, Gordon and Moreton, with the Hon Matthew Moreton. They won a contract to build a telegraph line to Cape York in Queensland, the northernmost point of the Australian continent. It was hard work over difficult terrain and took two years, 1885 to 1887, to complete.

While in Queensland he was appointed a Justice of the Peace, became a Captain in the Mercantile Marine and he married in Brisbane in 1889. However, his lust for adventure and his engineering skills took him to the other side of the country as a mining agent, and he ended up at Cue, a remote goldrush town in Western Australia, 400 miles north east of Perth. It was there that he died in 1899, aged 49.

Robert Leckie, a founding member of Queen's Park, died on a remote farmstead in South Africa. He played an important role in the club's early development, and was in the team which lifted the first Scottish Cup in 1874, scoring the clinching goal with a left foot shot. His only appearance for Scotland was in the first international, but he was well regarded as a player, and impressed DD Bone with his unique style of running: 'Comparatively short of stature and powerfully knit together, with splendidly moulded limbs, Leckie was one of the most tenacious forwards. While dribbling past an opponent with the ball at his toe, his peculiarity asserted itself in such a way that, once seen, could never be forgotten. When he obtained possession of the ball, he guarded his body with extended arms drooping from his side, with the back of his hands in front of the thighs, and thus formed a barrier to an opponent who attempted to tackle or take the ball from him.'[12]

This Queen's Park team from 1874 included five men who had played for Scotland in the first international against England two years earlier. They are all in the front row: (from left) Robert Leckie, Joseph Taylor, James J Thomson, James B Weir and William M Mackinnon.

After giving up football, Leckie sailed for South Africa, arriving in Port Elizabeth, a major trading port at that time, known as 'the Liverpool of the Cape'. However, it is not clear why he ended his days at Olifants Bosch in the Mankazana valley, about 130 miles to the north of Port Elizabeth; there was a Scottish community there, a collection of farmsteads with a tiny Presbyterian Church. He was clearly doing all right, as he left a chest containing clothing, a few books and a gold watch and chain, all to the value of 15 pounds 18 shillings. He may simply have gone to try and recover his health as the valley had a particularly dry climate and was thought to be good for treating tuberculosis. News of his death took over a month to reach home, and was confirmed by a notice inserted by his mother in the *Glasgow Herald* on the last day of 1886.

Leckie was not the first footballer to die in South Africa, although he had nothing in common with an Old Etonian who met a sudden end, killed by a bolt from the blue.

Thomas Nevile Carter had Eton College in his blood, being born at the school[13], where his father was a Fellow of Eton. An outstanding footballer, he was selected in the wall and field elevens and appointed Keeper of the Field in 1870; he was also the school Fives champion, and no doubt took pride in recording his own achievements as he was editor of the *Eton College Chronicle*. He was even fondly remembered by one of the younger boys: 'Carter was a merciful fagmaster, and I have no recollection of being caned by him.'[14]

What happened after he left Eton in 1871 is a blank sheet. According to the *Eton Register*, he went to Oxford University and was an awarded an MA at Queen's College, but the college has confirmed this is a mistake, due to confusion with a Thomas Nelson Carter of Cumberland. The *Register* was, however, precise in recording Carter's demise, killed by lightning on 16 November 1879 in South Africa (one edition specifies the Transvaal); why he was in the country during the Zulu Wars is a mystery waiting to be solved.

The last of the lonely graves belongs to Edward Vincent Ravenshaw, who is included in this book almost by accident, and was unfortunate enough to end his life through an accident as well. An excellent schoolboy sportsman, in the cricket and football elevens at Charterhouse, he may simply have been intending to watch several of his school's sporting heroes, such as Nepean and Hooman, play in the last of the unofficial internationals in February 1872.

He had no family links to Scotland but when Scotland's makeshift team found itself short of numbers, he was asked by team captain Montague Muir Mackenzie, an Old Carthusian, to play as an emergency substitute. This was the highlight of Ravenshaw's short football career, as he only played occasionally after leaving school and worked as a bank clerk in Malvern.

When he was offered the chance to become a tea planter in Assam, north-east India, he jumped at the opportunity, but the poor soul drowned in 1880 while attempting to save a friend's life. He and two other young planters were travelling by boat on the small but fast-flowing River Katakhal when one of them, a non-swimmer, fell in. His brave rescue failed and both were swept away in the strong current, their bodies found two days later, a mile downstream in a whirlpool. Ravenshaw was buried in the town of Silchar; a memorial painting was placed in Charterhouse school chapel but unfortunately it seems to have disappeared.

Men who left their mark

Many of the pioneers were fortunate enough to leave a legacy from their wanderings abroad, sometimes in surprising ways: having a toad named after you might not be everyone's idea of an accolade, but for Harold Ferguson it was the crowning glory of a lifetime's devotion to natural history.

Born into the London establishment, his father specialised in obstetrics and held the position of *physician-accoucheur* to Queen Victoria, assisting at the births of her children. Ferguson was educated at Eton until he was 16, then spent two years at Wimbledon (which played football under rugby rules) to prepare him for the entrance exams to the army. He was an outstanding pupil and came fifth in the 1869 exam to the Royal Military Academy at Woolwich, and duly obtained a commission in the Royal Artillery two years later. While at Woolwich he learned association football, and was selected for Scotland in the last couple of unofficial internationals.

However, Captain Ferguson resigned his commission in 1874[15] to take up a post in India as English tutor to the three Princes of Travancore, and later was appointed as second-in-command of the Nair Brigade of native troops maintained by the Maharajah of Travancore.

Ferguson's toad, an unusual accolade for a footballer

These roles allowed him to indulge his passion for natural history, and in 1894 he became director of the Trivandrum Museum and Public Gardens, developing and caring for its collections of animals, birds and plants. On expeditions into the country, he gathered numerous specimens which were sent to the British Museum, discovered the Travancore evening brown butterfly, and achieved a kind of immortality by having Ferguson's toad, *bufo scaber*, named after him. He was duly elected a Fellow of both the Linnean Society and the Zoological Society, and on retiring to London in 1904, he devoted himself to the Gardens at Regent's Park, serving on the Zoological Society's Council.

Only two of the early footballers are thought to be immortalised in a statue. One is that of Quintin Hogg in Langham Place, central London, showing him with two young boys, one holding a football, to mark his role as an educationalist and philanthropist. Hogg, who made two appearances for Scotland in unofficial internationals, was such an enthusiastic footballer that he was still playing competitively in the FA Cup with Hanover United at the age of 38, and turned out for 'Old Quintinians' in 1902 so that he could claim to have played fifty years of 'footer'.

This medal was struck in honour of Quintin Hogg, the 'Poor Boy's Friend'

Following Hogg's sudden death in 1903 – he suffocated in carbon monoxide fumes from a faulty heater while taking a bath – the statue was erected by members of the Polytechnic, which he had founded. Hogg's life was also remembered by the striking of commemorative medals, and in 1910 the Quintin Hogg Memorial Ground was opened at Chiswick; it still serves today as the sporting headquarters of the University of Westminster.

The other footballer statue is far away in Malaysia, *pictured left*. It commemorates Robert Sandilands Frowd Walker to mark his contribution to the formative years of the Malay states. Walker first saw the light of day in Chester Castle where his soldier father was serving as ordnance storekeeper, and attended Brentwood School, alongside several other early footballers. He played football for Clapham Rovers while gaining his commission at Sandhurst, and put his goal-scoring talents to good use with four goals in three matches for the unofficial England side. He then joined the 28th North Gloucestershire Regiment in 1872 and although his military duties took him far away from English football, he was not entirely lost to the game as he introduced football to Taiping, organising a team and donating the Ship Trophy for local competition (he also presented a challenge cup for polo teams).

This statue of RSF Walker stands in Taiping *(courtesy of Muzium Perak)*

Changing his surname to Frowd-Walker, he came to prominence in the suppression of the Perak rebellion in the late 1870s and was duly appointed to lead the Sikh police in Perak. He led the force for over a decade and then, in 1896, formed the Malay States Guides (within the Indian Army) and was appointed British Resident of Perak. Among his non-military achievements, he organised the transformation of an old mining site into the picturesque Taiping Lakes Gardens. A statue of him was erected by public subscription in 1912 with the support of the Sultans of Perak and Johore, and it now stands outside Perak Museum in Taiping, with an extensive plaque detailing his accomplishments.

He returned to England after retirement, with the rank of Lieutenant-General, but was recalled to military duties during the First

World War, acting until his death as the Commandant of the Alexandra Palace Prisoner of War Camp.

A memorial of a different kind belongs to Edward Bowen, a Harrow schoolmaster who wrote a football song that is still sung today. Bowen, born in Ireland, not only played for England in the first unofficial international, he then went on to win the FA Cup twice with Wanderers, the second time the day before his 37th birthday. He had been an active sportsman while at Cambridge University in the 1850s, taking part in rowing, skating and walking, his greatest feat being to walk from Cambridge to Oxford, about 84 miles, in 26 hours.

Edward Bowen dedicated his life to Harrow

He was appointed a Classics master at Harrow in 1859, and remained in post for the rest of his life, running a boarding house from 1864. He was founder of the 'Modern Side' at the school which gave a greater emphasis to languages, science and history rather than classical subjects, and was credited with introducing football competitions for younger boys. A keen military historian, shortly after his international appearance, in the summer of 1870 he travelled across France to follow in the tracks of the victorious German army in the Franco-Prussian war.

Bowen was a prolific writer of songs, including the anthem *Forty Years On* (1872), which remains the Harrow school song to this day, and captures the ambience of school football:

Routs and discomfitures, rushes and rallies,
Bases attempted and rescued and won,
Strife without anger, and art without malice –
How will it seem to you forty years on?

God give us bases to guard or beleaguer,
Games to play out whether earnest or fun,
Fights for the fearless, and goals for the eager,
Twenty, and thirty and forty years on.

He dedicated his life to Harrow and had hopes of being appointed headmaster but it never happened. Shortly before he was due to retire, he died suddenly of heart failure while on a cycling holiday in the south of France.

On the other side of the world, a street in Brisbane is named in memory of Scottish footballer Gilbert Primrose, although the connection is not immediately obvious. He was born on the Scottish estate of his grandfather, the 4th Earl of Rosebery, and now Rosebery Terrace runs through what used to be the grounds of Primrose's home in the Australian city. (There is an international echo as the 5th Earl of Rosebery was patron of the Scottish FA, and the national team played on occasion in his racing colours, primrose and rose.)

Educated at Trinity College, Glenalmond, Primrose went to Australia in 1873 with his brother Francis, and settled at Emu Creek, near Brisbane. There, they founded a mineral water bottling operation, the Helidon Spa Water Company, and Gilbert played a prominent role at a time when Queensland was a colony in its own right (it only became part of Australia in 1901): he was appointed a JP, made a Captain in the Queensland Scottish Rifles and the Queensland Defence Force, and represented Queensland at the Greater Britain Exhibition held at Earl's Court, London in 1899. He retired to England in 1909.

Other pioneers left their mark in more subtle ways, by committing themselves to colonial life, but it was not always easy. When Ned Kelly murdered three of his town's policemen, Charles Chenery must have wondered what he had let himself in for as he had arrived in Mansfield, Victoria, just weeks before.[16] Undaunted by the activities of the notorious outlaw nearby, the former footballer settled there for the rest of his life.

Best known for his football prowess, the only player to represent England in the first three full internationals, Chenery was the son of a gentleman farmer in Berkshire. He had had an early introduction to life in the colony when his father took the family in 1860 to Victoria, where two sisters were born, but they then came home. Chenery was educated at Marlborough Royal Free Grammar School, where he was in the same year as Frederick Chappell, and both followed a similar path on leaving school, coming to London where they took part in steeplechases and indulged in all sorts of sport.

Chenery played football for Wanderers and Crystal Palace, but remained keen on track events as a member of London Athletic Club, and acted as secretary of the first Wanderers FC sports in 1871. A good cricketer, he also played a dozen matches for Surrey. The lure of a return to Australia proved too strong, and he emigrated permanently in 1878, arriving in Hobson's Bay in September that year. He settled in Mansfield, where relatives were already based, became a cattle station manager, brought up a family and died there in 1928.

Over in New Zealand, Thomas Southey Baker devoted his life to teaching. He had been the outstanding athlete of his generation at Lancing College, not just in the cricket and football teams but also twice crowned *victor ludorum* in sports, and took up rowing at Oxford University with such success that he rowed in the Boat Race for three successive years. However, having played once for England in an unofficial football international, he was lost to British sport after emigrating to New Zealand in 1873; it was not an easy journey, as his ship, the *Dallam Tower*, was dismasted on the voyage.

Baker had planned to enter the New Zealand flax industry, but found it in such a parlous state that instead he established a private prep school at French Farm, near Christchurch and devoted the rest of his life to teaching. Keeping up his sport, he won the athletic sports championship at Timaru in 1878, and represented Canterbury against the first Australian cricket team to visit New Zealand in 1881.

In 1890, he was appointed as a teacher at Christ's College, Tasmania, but returned to New Zealand after two years and established Goodwood House prep school in Otago. In 1896 he became manager of a boarding-house at the Boys' High School of Dunedin, with the right to conduct his own school on the premises, and remained there until his death in 1902.

Colonial experiences

James Kirkpatrick, captain of Scotland's first unofficial teams, spent his first few years in Canada, still a British colony, where his father was a pioneer. In 1834, Charles Sharpe Kirkpatrick opened the first general store in the small Ontario town of New Hamburgh, and over the succeeding decade he married and had four children there, including James. Charles brought the family home to Scotland in 1844 when he succeeded his father as Baronet Kirkpatrick of Closeburn.

James never did return to the land of his birth. Brought up mainly in London, he joined the Civil Service early in 1861 as a temporary clerk in the Admiralty, and rose to become Private Secretary to the First Lord of the Admiralty. He had an unusually lengthy football career, playing for Civil Service and Wanderers from 1866, often as goalkeeper, with occasional matches for 1ˢᵗ Surrey Rifles. Elected to the FA committee in 1868, a position he held for four years, he joined Arthur Kinnaird in selecting the Scotland team in 1870, and took the role of team captain. He concluded his playing days by winning the FA Cup with Wanderers in 1878, the day after his 37th birthday, despite breaking an arm during the game.

He remained involved in football as President of Dulwich FC in the 1880s, and regularly acted as umpire at their matches. Kirkpatrick was also a good cricketer, a fast round-hand bowler for Civil Service and West Kent, and could throw a cricket ball 98 yards, twice winning first prize at the Civil Service Sports.

His accession to the baronetcy turned on a series of unfortunate events. First his father, 6th Baronet, died while travelling at La Libertad in El Salvador, then his elder brother Thomas keeled over while on his yacht in Dover Harbour. James became 8th Baronet Kirkpatrick in 1880, but he was not prepared for the expense and in February 1890 was declared bankrupt with over £11,000 of debts (and promptly suspended from his job at the Admiralty). He blamed his insolvency on paying off his brother's debts and having to support various family members, but was able to secure his release the following month by offering just £250 for distribution to his creditors.

He had a rather calmer start to life in the Empire than John Inglis, born in India, where his father was commander of the 32nd Regiment. The Inglis family found themselves caught up in the Mutiny of 1857 and young John celebrated his fourth birthday under attack in the Residency at Lucknow. Unlike many hundreds of their compatriots, they survived the ordeal and his father, Lieutenant Colonel Sir John Inglis, earned the title of 'the defender of Lucknow'; his mother wrote a book about their experiences.[17] The lifting of the siege should have been the end of their troubles, but they survived a shipwreck on the way home to the UK.

Having come through the Mutiny with his family unscathed, Inglis was more fortunate than William Lindsay, whose parents were murdered at Cawnpore. In the spirit of the times, though, he was one of three orphaned boys to be admitted to Winchester school[18], where he learned to play football. With a strong Scottish heritage – his father was born in Dundee, his grandfather was Provost of the city – he played for Scotland in all five unofficial internationals, but curiously was also capped by England in 1877, despite having no birth link.

Concluding this chapter is a man who did not emigrate, but travelled the world; in another era, Walter Paton might have worked for *Lonely Planet*. He was captain of football for two successive years at Harrow, earning him a call to play for England in the second unofficial international while still at school, and he represented Oxford University in the 1873 FA Cup final.

His job as honorary secretary of the Central Emigration Society, which included a position as publications editor at the Emigrants' Information Office, allowed him to voyage extensively around the world. In his mission to induce people to emigrate, Paton wrote numerous handbooks such as *The Handy Guide to Emigration to the British Colonies* and more specific guides to living conditions in places from Newfoundland to New South Wales. However, although he devoted his life to encouraging Britons to meet the demand for labour in our dominions and colonies, he always returned home and never followed his own advice.

---

[1] Dr Julius Klingner, born 1810 in Dresden, came to Scotland as a boy and graduated from Aberdeen University.

[2] Publishers of the *Glasgow Post Office Directory*

[3] DD Bone, *Scottish Football Reminiscences*, p31

[4] Bill Nye, *The Laramie Boomerang*, July 1881 and republished in *Forty Liars and Other Lies* (1883)

[5] *Progressive Men of the State of Wyoming*, p287-289.

[6] John Kerr, a mathematical lecturer at the Free Church Training College in Glasgow, published one set of findings in 1875, which became known as the Kerr Effect. The Kerr Cell was used in early televisions and to this day, the Kerr Medal is the highest award for scientists working in electro-optics.

[7] Manuscript letter by William Ker, dated 1925

[8] *Scottish Football Reminiscences*, p31

[9] She was known as Lizzie but seems to have changed it herself to Lily after her marriage.

[10] George Ker, born 26 February 1860 in Glasgow, died on his 62nd birthday at Yakima.

[11] *Scottish Football Reminiscences,* p28.

[12] *Scottish Football Reminiscences,* p28.

[13] There is, in fact, no record of his birth but he was certainly christened there in September 1851.

[14] Quoted in *A memoir of William Edmund Smyth: first Bishop of Lebombo 1893-1912*

[15] He remained on the reserve, and returned to service in 1914 as a captain in the London Rifle Brigade.

[16] Chenery arrived on 20 September; the Ned Kelly murders took place on 26 October.

[17] Julia Inglis, *The Siege of Lucknow: a Diary* (1892).

[18] The other orphaned boys were William Franklin Mawe and Henry Fisher Heathcote.

Chapter 7

GOOD SPORTS AND BAD SORTS

Thugs, bankrupts and gentlemen

Footballers can be model citizens, outstanding sportsmen with strong religious convictions. They are also subject to human frailties and can turn out to be nasty pieces of work. The early internationalists provided a cross-section of all that was good and bad.

THE COLONIAL Office was horrified: 'One can hardly imagine such fiendish cruelty in an English officer as to rub salt into the man's bleeding back.'

He wasn't an officer, he wasn't even English; but Robert Copland-Crawford was certainly guilty of the brutal killing of one of his servants. The Harrow-educated former Scotland player, the man who scored the first goal in international football, was locked up in a Sierra Leone jail for his crime.

It is a long way back from Freetown to London, and Copland-Crawford must have wished he could have started all over again. Twenty years earlier, on a spring day in 1870, he was cheered wildly as his kick found the goal in the first England v Scotland match. Ahead of him he had sporting glory, a windfall inheritance and a decorated military career, but he had thrown it all away. Footballers going off the rails? It is nothing new.

Born in Elizabeth Castle on Jersey, where his career soldier father was stationed in 1852, he was christened Robert for his father, Erskine Wade for his grandmother. His Irish-born father was General Robert Fitzgerald Crawford of the Royal Regiment of Artillery, his mother Jean came from a Scottish military family.[1]

General Crawford had a lengthy military career but never saw active service through postings to Jersey, Ireland, Belgium, France and Cape of Good Hope. Latterly, his wife remained in Scotland where three more children were born (and Robert received his early schooling); on retiring, he joined them for a while at Mavisbush House in Lasswade, just outside Edinburgh, before they took possession of a new home in Harrow towards the end of 1863. They called it Erskine House.

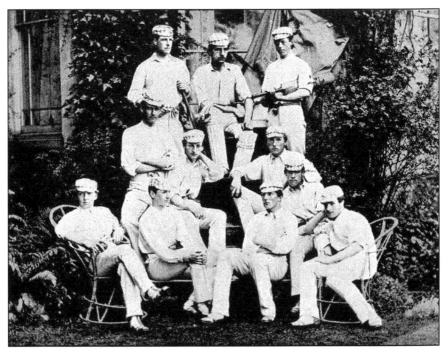

Robert Crawford (standing, top left) not only scored a goal for Scotland, he was also in this Harrow cricket eleven in 1871 which took on Eton at Lord's. Future England international Courtenay Welch is in the front row, second right.

General Crawford wanted to take advantage of an educational opportunity for his sons, as at that time the inhabitants of Harrow were allowed free admission to the school, without a competitive entry exam. Meanwhile, he became friendly with two spinster neighbours and local benefactors, the Copland sisters, who shared his evangelical persuasion. When one of them, Frances, died in 1870 she left £2,000 to Mrs Crawford; then when Anne Copland died aged 80 two years later, she bequeathed her house, Sudbury Lodge, together with 100 acres, to the Crawford family with the stipulation that they add Copland to their name. It was too good an opportunity to miss and the family surname was duly amended to Copland-Crawford in September 1872.

Robert had left school a year earlier, having played for Scotland in four of the five unofficial matches, although his most memorable sporting experience was probably batting for Harrow against Eton at Lords in the summer of 1871, a major event on the social calendar which attracted a crowd of over 20,000. After leaving school, he played football for Wanderers in 1871-72 and was in the team for the FA Cup semi-final against Queen's Park but not for the final. He appears to have given up football by 1873.

His father became president of Wembley Cricket Club, and Robert captained the team in 1872; he also played cricket for the MCC and was described as 'a fine player all round, often most brilliant, though apt to flag, generally plays the game thoroughly'.

After trying his hand briefly as a wine merchant, early in 1874 he gained a commission with the 4th battalion, 60th Rifles (later the King's Royal Rifle Corps), without first attending the Royal Military College at Sandhurst, which infers it was by sitting an entrance exam. It was a measure of his family's affluence and social position that he joined such a fashionable regiment, as a junior officer's pay was generally reckoned to be inadequate, on its own, to cover outgoings.

He progressed well, and was soon made 2nd Lieutenant, then Lieutenant in January 1876 (while in Ireland), and later that year travelled with the battalion to India. In February 1879 he transferred to the 2nd battalion at Meerut, heading on to Afghanistan (which the British had invaded in 1878) where he saw action in the Afghan War. He was in the Kandahar Field Force, part of the time as Orderly Officer to Brigadier General Richard Barter, under the overall command of Lt Gen Sir Donald Stewart. They marched through the Bolan Pass to Quetta and on to Kandahar, then a few weeks later to Ghazni, reaching Kabul in April 1880. On the way, he fought as a staff officer at the battle of Ahmed Khel and was mentioned in dispatches.

The British force occupied the Afghan capital, then news arrived in August that the garrison at Kandahar was under siege, and this prompted the sensational march under General Sir Frederick Roberts back to Kandahar. The 60th Rifles was one of three regiments which retraced their steps of four months previously, part of a force of 10,000 men and 7,500 followers who covered an astonishing 314 miles in three weeks, in temperatures that ranged from 105F in the day to freezing at night.

Lt Copland-Crawford was present at the Battle of Kandahar, where the Ayub Khan's Afghan Army was defeated, then took part in the final action, under General Charles MacGregor, a punishment expedition against the hostile Marri tribe in the south east of the country. He was awarded the specially struck 'Kabul to Kandahar' medal (also known as the Roberts Star) and the Afghan Medal, and his proud father submitted extracts from his letters home for publication in the *Harrow Gazette*. When the campaign finished in November, he rejoined his regiment at Meerut and sailed with it to South Africa, finally returning to the UK late in 1881.

The hero was married in London in August 1882 to Nellie Steuart, and they had a daughter, Helen, a year later. However, the marriage was clearly a disaster as they were divorced[2] shortly after Helen was born, prompting Robert to get as far away as possible. He requested a voluntary transfer to his regiment's 3rd battalion, sailing with them in November 1883 for Egypt and on to Sudan's Red Sea coast, where he took part in the attack on Osman Dinga, the Mahdist commander. He received both the Egyptian Medal and the Khedive of Egypt's Khedivial Star for his part in the campaign, but in August 1884, Lt Copland-Crawford suddenly resigned his commission and came home.

Clearly, despite his impeccable army record, something was seriously amiss, as he was fourth in seniority among the lieutenants of his regiment (second in his battalion) and could have expected promotion before too long. He had lost his wife and his military career within the space of a year.

He kept quiet at the family home, perhaps recuperating from illness, then in 1888 he was appointed to a local command with the frontier police in Sierra Leone, dealing with general police matters and customs. It was such an unattractive job that a colonel of the West India Regiment said he 'was not likely to let one of his officers undertake such a thankless and unprofitable task,' and it appears Copland-Crawford took on the role either through desperation or as some kind of personal penance. Regardless, he was the only man available and the Colonial Office admitted it was a 'somewhat doubtful policy to send a man without African experience down to such a hotbed of disturbance – apparently there was no help for it.'[3]

Although it was a civilian post, he styled himself as Captain Copland-Crawford when he arrived at the coastal trading post of Sulymah (now Sulima) on 17 September 1888. He was put in charge of a force of 77 men in the Sierra Leone constabulary, in their blue serge tunics and fez, and tasked with maintaining peace and order. He was supposed to come under the direction of Sir James Hay, Governor of Sierra Leone, but could not contain himself and, without authority,

84

used his military experience to take unilateral action against a notorious local warlord called Mackiah, who had occupied the town of Jehoma. After Copland-Crawford's force recaptured the town, in the course of which they killed 131 'warboys', the Colonial Office gave the action a cautious welcome: 'an excellently managed affair ... does great credit to Mr Crawford and the police ... no doubt exceeded his instructions but he was successful.'

Lord Knutsford, the Colonial Secretary, was not so sure and wrote 'however successful, it will not do to have subordinates acting independently,' but Copland-Crawford was given tacit approval to keep going. In fact, after he burned the village of Bahama as a punishment (it was empty at the time), Knutsford informed Hay that Copland-Crawford was in line to be recommended for the CMG (Companion of the Order of St Michael and St George).

When Hay arrived at Sulymah on 26 December, he sent Copland-Crawford on another mission against Mackiah, at the head of 75 police and 800 men who promptly captured the stronghold of Fahima after just an hour of fighting. So far, so good, but then Copland-Crawford started to behave strangely, hallucinating that Mackiah was lurking in the shadows, and was reported to have said 'I am afraid I am going out of my mind'. He was diagnosed with a disorder of the liver, and occasional paralysis of extremities.

At the end of February 1889 his life fell apart when he was accused of murder. Copland-Crawford claimed £84 had been stolen from his house (he said at his trial that the money was intended to set up a school at Sulymah), and employed a local man to find the thief by drawing a hot iron across the hand of suspects to extract a confession. Suspicion fell on a hammock carrier, but he in turn accused his personal servant, a 17-year-old boy called Walker.

On Copland-Crawford's orders, Walker was flogged three times, interrupted by questioning, and salt was rubbed into his open wounds. Witnesses later said they tried to intervene, but Copland-Crawford carried out a mock execution with a blank round. Next morning, with Walker handcuffed to a bedstead, he was further questioned and when he continued to deny any knowledge of the theft, Copland-Crawford called him a liar and punched him in the face. Not long afterwards, the boy was reported to be passing blood and, with no medical attention, he died the next day.

The coroner returned a verdict of unlawful killing, and Lord Knutsford ordered that Copland-Crawford – although clearly a sick man

– be charged with murder, later reduced to manslaughter. After a one month trial, in which he claimed that the salt was for antiseptic purposes, he was found guilty by the mainly local jury and sentenced to 12 months in prison. At a time when the death penalty was regularly imposed on native men, this may seem like a light sentence, but it was highly unusual for a British official to be convicted at all.

In view of Copland-Crawford's attacks of paralysis he was repatriated and, although it was intended he should serve his sentence in Liverpool, the senior surgeon at Walton Prison agreed to a remission of his sentence on medical grounds. He was free to return home. The matter was hushed up and may have ended there, but a condemnation of his behaviour was published in the *Anti-Slavery Reporter and Aborigine's Friend*. This in turn prompted a lengthy debate about his conduct in the House of Commons in June 1890, with Allanson Picton MP revealing a catalogue of atrocities by Copland-Crawford, including 'the slaughter of an indefinite number of people in several native towns, the burning of six or eight towns, and punishments inflicted of a cruel character on natives'. He concluded by saying the whole affair was 'inconsistent with morality and Christianity'.[4]

By then, Copland-Crawford was convalescing at Sudbury Lodge, but he never recovered his health and died there in May 1894 after a stroke. He was buried at St John's Church, Wembley, where there is a stained glass window in his father's memory, but few people were minded to commemorate the goal-scoring hero. However, there are echoes of the family in the area, with Copland Community School and Crawford Avenue, just a stone's throw away from Wembley Stadium.

Robert was joined in the Scotland team for the last two of the unofficial matches by his younger brother, Fitzgerald Hamilton Crawford. The first of the family to be born north of the border, his profile was considerably lower than Robert's but he did share some of his sporting talent. He played football in 1871/72 for Harrow Chequers (even though he did not attend Harrow) and once for Wanderers.

He appears to have been educated privately and was clearly intelligent, being elected a Fellow of the Royal Geographical Society at the tender age of 24. This must have been his consuming interest, as in the 1881 census he gave this as his occupation. From then until his death in 1894 he was apparently a lodger with Mrs Frances Leyland at 6 Hans Place, Sloane Street, which would have been unremarkable in itself, but Mrs Leyland was a figure of some renown: her husband was a wealthy patron of the American artist James Whistler, who painted her portrait and was rumoured to have had an affair with her, one of the factors in the Leylands' high profile divorce.

Assault with a chicken, and other difficulties

A number of other international footballers suffered problems in their lives, including marital and financial difficulties.

Alexander Bonsor led a philandering life of leisure, having been born into a privileged existence which began at Polesden Lacey in Surrey, now a National Trust property[5]. He was educated at Eton and inherited a substantial shareholding in the family brewing business, becoming a director of Combe & Co (a forerunner of Watneys) which gave him the wherewithal to enjoy himself. An excellent footballer, he played in four of the first five FA Cup finals, winning with Wanderers in 1872 and 1873, then twice on the losing side for Old Etonians. Having featured in the last of the unofficial internationals, he was capped twice for England, scoring the second goal in 1873, then as goalkeeper in 1875.

Bonsor had a weakness for women, in particular French-speaking ones, and scandalised his family. He lived for at least ten years with a Belgian called Marie Charlotte whom he described as his wife, even though there is no evidence they were married, and according to the 1891 census they had a daughter called Edwina. Then in 1893 he married Jeanne Marie David, a French woman who left him after two years, claiming in a high-profile divorce case that he would regularly come home the worse for drink, threw things at her (including a chicken) and assaulted her. She also accused him of adultery with at least two other women. By the time she obtained her divorce he had moved to Belgium, where he married again, and he lived near Brussels until his death in 1907.

Financial troubles hit John Cockerell, who was unusual among the early footballers, being a clerk with a coal merchant. However, this was at a time when coal was one of Britain's greatest industries, with the potential to be hugely profitable.

Cockerell was a prominent sportsman in the 1860s, culminating in two selections for the unofficial England team and a role as team selector in recognition of his position as club captain of Brixton. He had started in football with Crystal Palace, earning representative honours for the Surrey & Kent side in 1868, and three times for Surrey. He also had quite a reputation as an athlete, running for Brixton AC and South Norwood AC; famously he won a quarter mile race against WG Grace at

Blackheath Sports in June 1868, and was reported as winning events in Devon, presumably while on holiday, in the summers of 1868 and 1869. He rowed on the Thames and played cricket for Crystal Palace.

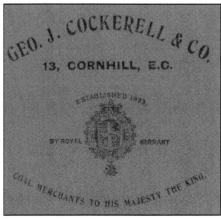

Cockerell's Coal had a royal warrant

He worked for his uncle's company, George Cockerell & Co, which dominated the London coal trade and proudly advertised its credentials as suppliers to the Queen and to the Royal Family. Having learned all he could about the coal business, in 1882 he struck out on his own in direct competition to the family firm, placing adverts in *The Times*. It was a disastrous move, and less than a year later the adverts stopped suddenly; the business foundered and he had to file for bankruptcy. Happily, it appears he was forgiven and accepted back into the parent company, continuing to work with them for many years.

Another who went bankrupt was James Mein, who played for Scotland in the first rugby international. He ran the family farm at Hunthill, just outside Jedburgh in the Scottish borders, and when he inherited the neighbouring property of Scraesburgh in 1890 from his uncle, he assumed his uncle's names to become James Andrew Whitelock Mein. Unfortunately this led him into financial difficulties and the farms were sequestrated in 1914; he managed to discharge himself from his debts the following year but the land was lost for ever, and he died three years later.

Men of God

The ministry was a career choice for a number of young footballers, a reflection of Victorian times and the muscular Christian ethos of *mens sana in corpore sano*[6].

There can be few better introductions to the ministry than having a father who was chaplain to Queen Victoria, but Charles Nepean developed many other talents. By the time he was ordained he had more than proved himself on the sports field: at Charterhouse, he

88

was captain of football for three years and of cricket for two, and was asked to play for Wanderers while still at school. Nepean played four times for Scotland in the unofficial internationals, helped found the football club at Oxford University, won the FA Cup with them in 1874, and earned his blue in a victory over Cambridge. The *Morning Post* described him as 'One of the best players extant. No one, it is imagined, who witnessed his ability when at Charterhouse can forget his untiring energy and fine play.'[7] He was also a talented cricketer, winning a blue in 1873, also playing for Middlesex and for Gentlemen v Players.

Charles Nepean (seated left, with pads) was captain of cricket at Charterhouse, where this photo was taken in 1868. Also in this team were footballers TC Hooman (England), JF Inglis (Scotland) and William Wallace, who played for Wanderers and was Scotland's umpire in the third unofficial international. (*reproduced by kind permission of the Headmaster and Governors of Charterhouse*)

On leaving university, Nepean's sporting talent went to waste as when he was ordained in 1874, he gave up football on becoming curate in a Hampshire parish. Two years later he was appointed vicar of Lenham in Kent, holding the charge for the rest of his life. He kept out of the limelight, but bumped into an old friend in 1902. Quintin Hogg was visiting Hastings with a group of Polytechnic boys and was shocked to find his old team-mate suffering from cancer: 'I was recognised by Charlie Nepean, whom I knew as a charming young fellow five-and-thirty years ago, when he played in the International Scotch team under my captaincy.[8] I had not seen him for nearly thirty years, but he knew me in a moment, and I was grieved to find that he come down there to die, being afflicted with a hopeless attack of cancer. He was as bright and cheery as ever, and as full of pluck as when he shared with me the charge of the back division of the Scotch team.'[9]

Ironically, despite his illness, Nepean outlived his friend, as within weeks Hogg succumbed to carbon monoxide poisoning while taking a bath.

Nepean was in the same Oxford college cricket team as Arnold Kirke Smith, who made two appearances for Scotland in the unofficial internationals, thanks to a Scottish grandfather (who was also a minister), but was capped for England *against* Scotland in the first official game of 1872. He also won a blue and captained the Oxford University side in the FA Cup final of 1873.

Ordained in 1875, he was appointed curate at Biggleswade and Eaton Socon, then vicar of Somersham with Pidley and Colne, and finally rector of Boxworth from 1889, where he remained until his death. In the mould of a typical country vicar, he was keen on beekeeping.

A third Oxford-educated minister also excelled at football. Walpole Vidal was a precocious talent, being the youngest player, a 16-year-old Westminster schoolboy, when he was chosen for England in the first of the unofficial internationals. He was one of only three England players (along with Alcock and Lubbock) to play in all five unofficial games and was still under 20 when he won his only full cap in 1873. He played in the first three FA Cup finals, and scored the winner in the first ever Varsity match, giving Oxford a 1-0 victory over Cambridge on 30 March 1874. To do this, he dribbled the length of the pitch before shooting into the top corner with the entire Cambridge team on his heels: 'I can see today the corner I elected to shoot at and even now I feel a shiver of apprehension as I see the ball going much higher than I meant and only passing under the tape by about three inches.' Vidal was vicar of his home town, Abbotsham in Devon, from 1881 until his death.

Two footballing vicars who were at Cambridge University both won the FA Cup with Wanderers in 1873, in direct opposition to AK Smith and RWS Vidal. Henry Holmes Stewart was ordained in 1872, a year after he graduated from Trinity College, and embarked on a series of church appointments that would take him around the country. His first charge was as a curate in central London, but thereafter he was a vicar in Yorkshire, spent 20 years in Northamptonshire, then from 1898 until his retirement in 1934 he had charges in and around Cardiff.

Old Etonian Charles Thompson (whose surname became Meysey-Thompson in 1874) went on to further sporting achievements, winning an athletics blue at Cambridge in the hammer, and playing in the 1876 FA Cup final with Old Etonians. However, his working life was short: after being ordained he was curate at Whitby and St Pancras before an appointment as rector of Claydon, Bucks, in 1876. Suffering from poor health, he travelled to Utah to benefit from the dry heat, but died at Peoa in the Weber Canyon. He is buried in Mount Olivet Cemetery in Salt Lake City; there is also a memorial at the family mausoleum in Little Ouseburn, near York.

Football legends

For all the varying lifestyles and careers of the early international players, it must not be forgotten that some of them were enormously influential in developing football, and will be primarily remembered for devoting a substantial part of their lives to the sport. In particular, the triumvirate of Charles Alcock, Arthur Kinnaird and Charles Clegg dominated football administration for the first half century of the game, guiding the game from amateurism to professionalism.

You had to be tough to survive in football, and the great cricketer WG Grace once described Alcock playing for England against Scotland: 'In those days you were allowed to use your shoulders and the way Alcock used to knock over a fellow when he was trying to pass him I shall never forget.' His robust style was not always welcome, however, and Edgar Lubbock once took umbrage at a heavy charge, shouting: 'By God! Alcock, if you do that again I'll hack off your legs.'[10]

Alcock captained England in all five unofficial internationals and led Wanderers to the FA Cup in 1872, but only won one full cap for England as injury kept laying him low at crucial moments; he also refereed two FA Cup Finals. His greatest influence was off the field and he served as FA secretary from 1870-95, remaining on Council until his death in 1907. He was also responsible for writing much of the early history of football: he started as a reporter for *The Sportsman* and *The Field*, edited the *Football Annual* for almost forty years, wrote the classic *Football: Our Winter Game* (1874), published *Football: A Weekly Record of the Game* (1882-83), and wrote many other guides to the game.

Arthur Kinnaird, later Lord Kinnaird, was held to be 'without exception the greatest player of the day' according to Charles Alcock's *Football Annual*, and no wonder: he won the FA Cup five times and played in nine finals, which remains a record to this day. Having launched the unofficial series of internationals, he played once for Scotland in 1873 before the Scottish FA implemented a policy of home-based players only. He also had enormous influence as an FA committee member for a total of 55 years, having joined in 1868 and going on to serve as President from 1890 until his death in 1923.

Scotland international and team selector Arthur Kinnaird still holds the record for the most FA Cup final appearances (*courtesy of Rick Zimmerman*)

Kinnaird was probably more proud, however, of his record as a philanthropist. As a young man, he and Quintin Hogg had set up a ragged school in the east end of London, and as an ardent evangelical Kinnaird became head of national religious movements such as the YWCA and YMCA, and gave passionate support to an extraordinary number of charities, missions and good causes. He was appointed three times as Lord High Commissioner to the General Assembly of the Church of Scotland.

Charles Clegg succeeded Kinnaird as FA President in 1923, having been a committee member since 1886 and chairman of Council since it was formed in 1890. He had played for Sheffield, Sheffield Wednesday and other local clubs, and was chosen for England in the first official international in 1872; his brother William played in the return later that season. Having given up playing, Clegg refereed the 1882 and 1892 FA Cup finals and did much to promote the game in his home town: in 1888, he established the Clegg Trophy for Sheffield schools, thought to be the very first schools competition, and he served as President of both Sheffield clubs, United and Wednesday. A memorial bust was unveiled at Hillsborough in 1938, but is now missing.

---

[1] General Crawford (1809-1894) married Jean Dalrymple Anderson (1823-1896) in 1850 at Burntisland, Fife. For a detailed family history see *The Copland Crawfords of Wembley*, by Richard E Brock (1989).

[2] Nellie did not remarry, but when she died on 15 March 1918 she left £17,000 in her will, which implies she was well looked after in a divorce settlement.

[3] For further details, see Colonial Office archive at the Public Record Office: CO 267 Sierra Leone original correspondence; CO 268 entry books; CO 271 Official Gazette.

[4] *Hansard*, 2 June 1890

[5] The home was extensively remodelled in Edwardian times, and the future King George VI and Queen Elizabeth spent part of their honeymoon at Polesden Lacey in 1923.

[6] A healthy mind in a healthy body

[7] *Morning Post*, 22 February 1872

[8] Hogg did not, in fact, captain any of the Scotland teams.

[9] Ethel Hogg, *Quintin Hogg*, p360.

[10] *Fifty Years of Sport,* Vol 2, p67

Chapter 8

MATTERS OF IDENTITY

Making a name for themselves

In an age when class was all-important, only a gentleman could play amateur sport, and the right name could be one's social passport. While some footballers had little difficulty proving their aristocratic credentials, others indulged in a little gamesmanship.

FREDERICK CHAPPELL had an extraordinary range of talents. In sport, he was an international footballer, a champion boxer and rower, and played tennis at Wimbledon. He was intelligent enough to earn a good degree at Oxford, run a successful music publishing company, become a partner in a firm of solicitors, and stand as a candidate at a general election. Yet, somehow, he never seemed quite at ease with himself.

For a start, there was quite a saga over his name. Born plain Frederick Chappell, at Oxford University he was sometimes listed as Frederick M Chappell in official communications (the Brasenose College register even confused him with his father, Frederick Patey Chappell). He cannot have been happy with his surname as in some football team lines he used the pseudonym F McLean. Then in February 1873, half-way through his degree course, he formally changed his name to Frederick Brunning Maddison, as a reference to his maternal grandfather; it was generally used as a double-barrelled surname (his children and descendants were Brunning-Maddisons), but often he was FB Maddison. And just for a bit of variety, he varied his first name from Frederick to Frederic.

Born in London, Chappell was educated (alongside future England colleague Charles Chenery) at Marlborough Royal Free Grammar School, where he won a Somerset Scholarship to Brasenose College. As a footballer, having turned out for Scotland in one of the unofficial games, he played in attack for England in the first international of 1872, then won the FA Cup twice with Oxford University and Wanderers. He was selected again for England in 1876 but was unavailable.

The boxing medal won by FB Maddison, the former Frederick Chappell, in 1873 (*courtesy of Rita Wellstead*)

Chappell had a wealth of other sporting achievements. Having joined Kingston Rowing Club after leaving school, he continued rowing at Oxford with success: he won the Junior Sculls at the Metropolitan Regatta in 1870, and rowed for Oxford in the Henley Royal Regatta in 1871. In boxing, he won the Amateur Athletic Club heavyweight championship, the Marquis of Queensberry's Challenge Cup, in 1873, having been a beaten finalist in the middleweights two years earlier. Later, he played lawn tennis at Wimbledon, losing in the first round in 1880 to William Renshaw (who would go on to win 12 Wimbledon titles). And then he took up golf, and is recorded among entrants to the Open Championship at Prestwick in 1893, although he withdrew without hitting a ball.

His legal career began after graduating in Jurisprudence in 1874. He was called to the bar in 1876, but after seven years was disbarred at his own request to be a solicitor. He became senior partner in the firm of Maddison, Stirling and Humm, and even though he left in 1904 the company retained his name until the 1940s.

He had political ambitions and stood as a Gladstonite Liberal at Rochester in the general election of 1892, losing by 407 votes to the Conservative, Horatio Davies. In a bitter campaign, his wife was hit on the face by an oyster shell on her way to a hustings meeting, then the result was ruled void by a court on the grounds of corruption: Davies's agents had been buying beer and cigars for voters.[1] Maddison wisely decided not to stand at the by-election the following year,

Music was his passion, not surprisingly as his grandfather had founded Chappell & Co, the famous music publisher and piano manufacturer. Frederick became a director of a similar enterprise, Metzler & Co, where his legal expertise was useful in defending it in a copyright action. He married a young singer on the company's books,

Adela Tindal, in 1883 and they had two children, but for a musical couple it must have been heart-breaking that their son Noel was deaf.[2]

However, there was a scandal after he and his wife became close friends with the French composer Gabriel Fauré, who had signed a contract with Metzler & Co. Adela left her husband in 1898 to live with the composer in Paris. Even after the affair ended, she pursued a solo singing career in Germany, but as Brunning Maddison died in Berlin in 1907, where Adela was then working, it suggests they were reconciled.

Aristocratic leanings

A number of footballers acquired a title later in life, some earned for service to the nation, others were inherited.

Arthur Kinnaird did so because of tragic circumstances, having grown up without any expectation of succeeding to the family title. The family saga began when George, ninth Lord, was victim of a series of tragedies. First, his younger brother Graham drowned when the ship he commanded, HM Brig *Rapid*, was driven onto rocks in a storm in eastern Algeria; although his valiant efforts saved the lives of his crew, he went down with his ship. George's heir, Victor, was never in the best of health and died aged 11; and finally his second son, Charles, contracted malaria while on the Grand Tour and died in Naples in 1860, aged 17. These unfortunate events brought George's youngest brother Arthur into line for the succession (which he did in 1878) and in turn his son, Arthur Fitzgerald Kinnaird, became 11th Lord Kinnaird in 1887.

Henry Preston succeeded his father as 3rd Baronet Preston in 1891, together with possession of the large Gothic mansion where he was born, but had little time to enjoy his position as he died of scarlet fever and blood poisoning just six years later, aged 45.

Wingfield Malcolm, the fearsome MP who defended Scotland's lines resolutely in the first unofficial international, came from a family who had been Argyllshire landowners for centuries. He was 15th Laird of Poltalloch, described in 1878 as 'the beau ideal of a Highland chieftain,'[3] and elevated to the peerage when he was made Lord Malcolm of Poltalloch in 1896. However, he died childless six years later and the lordship became extinct; he was succeeded as Laird by his brother, whose descendants now live in Duntrune Castle.

Malcolm was an enthusiastic volunteer with the London Scottish, and Colonel of the Argyllshire Rifle Volunteers. He took part in shooting competitions from the early 1860s, regularly winning prize money and was Scotland's top scorer in the victorious 1869 Elcho Shield competition, and non-competing captain of the Scotland Eight which competed for the Shield in 1876. He was also a keen yachtsman, Commodore of the Royal Northern Yacht Club at Oban.

Kenneth Muir Mackenzie actually earned his title, after his older brother inherited the baronetcy of his father. A senior law officer, he had been Principal Secretary to the Lord Chancellor and Clerk of the Crown, with a notable highlight of his legal career coming when he led evidence for the prosecution at the trial of notorious murderer Hawley Harvey Crippen in 1910. In June 1915, on his 70th birthday, he was made 1st Baron Muir-Mackenzie (with a hyphen), but the title became extinct on his death as his only son predeceased him. In 1924 he became a Labour whip in the House of Lords and was made a Privy Councillor.

A name of two halves

Not everyone can have a title, and the next best thing for many of the early footballers was a double-barrelled surname, which they achieved for varying reasons ranging from marriage and inheritance to sheer vanity.

The Baillie-Hamilton brothers were generally referred to as plain Hamilton in football reports, but they followed the style of their father, an Admiral who was born a Baillie and added the Hamilton after marrying his heiress wife.

Henry Renny-Tailyour's surname derives from a merger between the Renny and Tailyour families in Montrose during the 18th century, although the name was not formally changed until the year of his birth. He deserves a special mention for representing Scotland at rugby in 1872, and at football in 1873; he remains the only Scot to have done so. In the latter match, he wore his rugby shirt with embroidered thistle, while the other players had a lion rampant on their chest.[4] He played for Royal Engineers in three FA Cup finals, finally winning the Cup in 1875 after two defeats, and also held the distinction of being the only double-barrelled player to represent Scotland until 2011, when Craig Mackail-Smith made his debut.

Renny-Tailyour was also a fine cricketer, captain of cricket at school and at the Royal Military Academy (where he also won the mile race, a feat repeated by his son Henry in 1912, two years before he was killed at Ypres). He reputedly made 54 centuries between 1867 and

1898, mainly for the RE team, including 331 not out v Civil Service in 1880, and also played for Kent, Gentlemen v Players (1874 and 1875) and Gentlemen of the South (1874).

With the Royal Engineers he had a varied career which included periods in Gibraltar and several years as an instructor of fortification and military engineering at Chatham. In 1891 he was appointed Commanding Engineer and Director of Military Works in New South Wales, where he published a pamphlet *The land forces of Australasia and their dispositions for war*. After retiring from the RE in 1899 with the rank of Brevet Colonel, he became managing director of Arthur Guinness & Son in Dublin.

The Muir Mackenzie family was created by the first baronet, who merged the Muir and Mackenzie estates in Perthshire, but when Kenneth was made a baron in 1916 he tinkered with the name by introducing a hyphen.

Crawford became Copland-Crawford in 1872, as already related, and a year later, Albert and Charles Thompson adopted a double-barrelled surname when their father was created baronet Meysey-Thompson, taking Meysey from his grandmother.

There were strange machinations for Robert Walpole Sealy Vidal, who called himself Walpole rather than Robert. The family name had been Sealy until 1842 when an inheritance from a relative carried a stipulation that the family surname must be changed to Vidal. This was done, and the children were given a middle name of Sealy. Walpole unilaterally decided to drop the Vidal in 1892 and revert to the Sealy surname, while other members of his family were not quite so brave and used a hyphenated Sealy-Vidal.

Others made small changes, probably for social reasons: Arnold Kirke Smith adapted his surname to Kirke-Smith while at Oxford University, RSF Walker transformed himself into Major Frowd-Walker while in Malaysia, and Reginald Courtenay Welch began calling himself R de Courtenay Welch.

Another who changed his name did so almost by accident. JC Smith appears in the first unofficial England team list, and regularly in football match reports for Westminster School, but this disguised his true identity. The initials were based on a phonetic rendering of his first name: he enrolled at the school as Julio, but his real name was the Italian spelling Giulio, which he reverted to in adult life. In fact, his full name was Giulio Cowley Tyler Smith, the son of a prominent surgeon,

Dr William Tyler Smith, who founded the Obstetrical Society of London and was a sub-editor of the *Lancet*.

Smith played football for Middlesex in November 1867 while still at school, and was also a talented athlete, winning the mile and the 100 yards. He became a tea and coffee merchant with the firm of John Cassell & Co (better known as publishers) of Fenchurch Street, London. He adapted his surname to Tyler-Smith, married but had no children, and spent his final years at Seaford, where his father had founded a convalescent hospital.

In search of identity

Inevitably, there remain mysteries about the early footballers, and as more historical records come on line perhaps they will be solved.

There were two students called Robert Munro at St Andrews University in 1871, and it has not been resolved conclusively which one was selected for Scotland in the first rugby international. The cap has sometimes been ascribed to the older of the two, but he left the university and was ordained as a minister in the summer of 1871; however, R Munro continued to appear in team lines until the end of 1873. The younger is the more likely candidate, particularly as he was a contemporary of other prominent university players of that era, but a definitive answer would be welcome.

In association football, it might be expected that someone who captained England on his international debut, played with distinction for Wanderers, and sat on the FA committee would be well known. Yet for all his sporting pedigree, Alexander Morten's background remains obscure.

In census returns, Morten reported that he was born in Paddington, central London, and gave an age that dates him to 1831 or 1832[5], but no confirmation has been found in parish records. When he married Flora Hedger in 1855 at St Peter's Church in Petersham, he gave his 'rank or profession' as gentleman on the marriage certificate, but put a line through the box for father's name. As a man of independent means, it is surprising that he was unable or unwilling to name his father; it is possible he was illegitimate with a private legacy, but this is speculation. When the announcement went in the *Morning Chronicle*, the only clue to his background was that he was living in Teddington. There appears nothing remarkable about the Morten's life thereafter: he and his wife set up home in Kensington Park and had two sons and four daughters, all baptised at the church of St John the Evangelist, Notting Hill.

His sporting career can be traced from 1860 when he played cricket for Kensington Park[6] and subsequently for Crystal Palace. The first mention of him playing football was for NNs of Kilburn in April 1863, already in his thirties, at a time when few men stayed active in sport beyond their twenties. Yet, despite his age, for the next ten years there was no stopping him on the football field, and he captained Crystal Palace as well as making numerous appearances for Wanderers. He won representative honours including a place in the first unofficial Scotland team, and was granted the captaincy of England against Scotland on his debut in March 1873. After a final selection for London against Sheffield in 1874 he appears to have retired, aged about 42.

Morten's unusual 'late blossoming' has prompted some football historians to query whether he has been correctly identified – particularly as there was another Alexander Morten who was born in Amersham in 1851, emigrated to the USA where he was a successful golfer, and died in New York in 1916. But Morten's direct descendants have confirmed the identification, and indeed they still hold his copy of the match card from the international in 1873.

He pursued a living as a stockbroker, with offices in Angel Court, and there are occasional references to Morten in the newspapers, generally as a broker for share issues. Alarmingly, he was accused of obtaining £1,000 by false pretences in 1875[7], but his wife came to court to explain he was 'utterly incapacitated' through illness, and the case seems to have been dropped. Otherwise he had an uneventful career and apart from being elected a Fellow of the Royal Colonial Institute in 1891 there are few clues to his life. He died in 1900, described simply as 'formerly of the stock exchange', and was buried in Kensal Green Cemetery.

The final whistle

Football is, of course, more than a matter of life and death, yet it is remarkable how many international players died young. It is perhaps indicative of different levels of prosperity between north and south that early death was much more prevalent among those who represented Scotland: five of the 1872 football team, four of the 1871 rugby team, and four of the unofficial internationalists did not live beyond 40; the comparative figures for England are one, two and one.

For those whose cause of premature death is known, the greatest scourge was tuberculosis. One of the more poignant cases was that of Scotland's Joseph Taylor, who played in the first six internationals and had three Scottish Cup winners' medals. When he gave up playing, he remained closely involved with Queen's Park, serving as its president. He worked as a clerk for a drapery wholesaler, got married and had four sons. Then, in the autumn of 1888 he was struck down with pleurisy and tuberculosis, and died at home in Victoria Terrace, close to Hampden Park. He was just 37 years old.

Memorial to Joseph Taylor in Cathcart Cemetery, Glasgow

The club rallied round and staged a benefit match against Third Lanark for his widow and children, attracting 7,000 spectators to Hampden Park. Not only did his family receive the gate receipts, Queen's Park then added a further £50. There was a macabre twist to the benefit match, as a few days before it was played, news came of the death of another former player with both clubs, Andrew Hillcoat; black armbands were worn in his honour.

Other early internationalists found more imaginative ways to die: TN Carter was struck by lightning, EV Ravenshaw drowned, Cuthbert Ottaway caught a chill while out dancing, Scotland rugby star JLH McFarlane developed a fatal fever after injuring his knee in a match, and his team captain WD Brown stepped in front of a train.

Happily, many lived to a ripe old age and some even shed light on the early days of football. As late as 1938 Thomas Hooman was interviewed about his playing days. An irascible Hooman, still wearing his blue, red and pink school tie, initially refused to speak to the young journalist who turned up on his doorstep until he realised that his visitor, Tibby Clarke, was a fellow Old Carthusian.[8] He talked mainly about the first FA Cup final, in which he played for Wanderers against Royal Engineers (he even claimed to have scored the winning goal, which his interviewer was too polite to contradict), but gave an insight into the physical nature of the game in 1872:

'Game hadn't been on ten minutes when one of their best men broke his collar bone in a throw-in.'

'He threw so hard?'

'No, no, in the scrum. When the ball went out of play, the first man to reach it took the throw. Not a bad idea, gave the crowd a bit of participation. I've lain there hugging the ball with four of the other side and half a dozen spectators in a heap on top of me.'

'You didn't have substitutes?'

'Good gracious, no. In that case it wasn't necessary. Plucky chap played on.[9] Made one feel a bit of a cad barging him. Still, *versa rota fortunae*, what?'

Six months later, Hooman passed away, but he was not quite the last of the international pioneers. While the events of this book may appear to belong to a different age, it is a sobering thought that there are people alive today who knew Jarvis Kenrick, who played for England in an unofficial international. He is best known as the man who scored the first ever goal in the FA Cup, for Clapham Rovers against Upton Park on 11 November 1871, but was a potent forward throughout the decade, and he later won the Cup three times with Wanderers, scoring in two of the finals.

Kenrick was a solicitor, based in Surrey at Pendell House, a spacious 17th century red brick mansion designed by Inigo Jones, where he and his wife brought up no fewer than nine daughters, supported by two governesses, seven servants and three gardeners. When the girls had all left home, he moved to Wimbledon, and his final years were spent with his daughter Audrey on the Sussex coast at East Blatchington.

He died there in January 1949, aged 96, and with his demise the story of the men who created international football came to an end.

---

[1] The corruption court case prosecution was led by two footballing barristers, Alfred Lyttelton and Tinsley Lindley, both of whom had played for England.

[2] Noel Brunning Maddison was one of the first deaf people to graduate from a British university, taking his degree at Imperial College, London, in 1910.

[3] *The Bailie*, 21 August 1878

[4] This can be clearly seen in the Scotland team photo taken in March 1873.

[5] A date of birth has been suggested in some publications as 15 November 1831, but the author is not aware that any records have been found to verify this.

[6] *Bell's Life,* 15 December 1861, provides a season overview.

[7] *Freeman's Journal*, 9 March 1875

[8] The interview was repeated by Clarke in *Punch*, 7 May 1980, p698.

[9] The injured player was Lieut EW Creswell, who played on despite being in severe pain.

Chapter 9

ASSOCIATION FOOTBALL BIOGRAPHIES

ALCOCK, Charles William

*England unofficial matches 1-5;
England internationalist.*
Born 2 December 1842 in
Bishopwearmouth, County
Durham; died 26 February 1907
in Brighton, Sussex.
Harrow (1855-59). Along with his
brother John, he was a founder
of the Forest Club in 1859; he
then founded and ran Wanderers
from 1864, captaining them to
victory in the inaugural FA Cup
in 1872. He also turned out for
many other clubs. Captained
England in all five unofficial
internationals but only won one
full cap in 1875, having been
selected for the previous three
but injured on each occasion.

Made numerous representative
appearances for London,
Middlesex and Surrey, also for
the North v South (1870). Joined
the FA committee in 1866,
secretary from 1870-95, remained
on Council until his death. He
refereed the FA Cup finals of
1875 and 1879, and was first
president of the Referees'
Association. A prolific journalist,
he was also secretary of Surrey
County Cricket Club.
Son of Charles Alcock, ship
builder, and Elizabeth Frances
Forster. Married Eliza Caroline
Ovenden in 1864, two sons and
six daughters.

BAILEY, William Heap

Scotland unofficial match 2.

Born 28 February 1847 in
Melbourne, Derbyshire; died 1
February 1926 in London.
Derby Mechanics Institution.
Played football for Civil Service
and Upton Park (which he
captained). Joined the Civil
Service in 1864, as assistant
book-keeper in the Science and
Art Department. Moved in 1866
to the Civil Service Commission
and in 1869 to the Paymaster
General's office. Joined Bass
brewers in Burton c1870,
subsequently becoming their
London manager. A keen rower,
he won several prizes with
Burton RC.
Son of William Heap Bailey and
Elizabeth Worrall. Married
Louisa Cartlidge in 1881, one son
and two daughters. *Image courtesy
Bill Bailey.*

**BAILLIE-HAMILTON, Charles
Robert**

Scotland unofficial match 1.

Born 24 September 1848 in
Greenwich, Kent; died 28 July
1927 in Taplow, Bucks.
Repton (1862-66). Played for
Civil Service and was a keen
athlete, regularly taking part in
the Civil Service Sports until
1874. A clerk to the Treasury
from 1868-89, he then became an
artist, living at Upland Place,
Preston, Lavenham, Suffolk.
Filed a patent for a velocipede in
1884 (*pictured below*). He left just
£71 in his will.

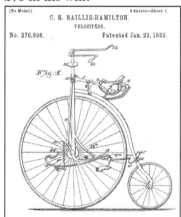

Son of Admiral William
Alexander Baillie-Hamilton and
Lady Harriet Hamilton. Did not
marry.

**BAILLIE-HAMILTON, William
Alexander**
Scotland unofficial match 1.
Born 6 September 1844 in
Brighton, Sussex; died 6 July
1920 in Sloane Street, London.
Harrow (1857-63). Played for Old
Harrovians and Civil Service,

and once for Wanderers in 1873. Joined the Colonial Office 1864, sent to America on 'secret service' three years later. Became a barrister in 1882, and was private secretary to the Secretary of State for the Colonies, chief clerk of the Colonial Office in 1896 and knighted the following year. In 1885 he published a novel in three volumes, *Mr Montenello, a romance of the civil service*, which may have been in part auto-biographical. When he retired in 1909, he wrote a memoir which revealed how the sleepy nature of the Colonial Office gave ample opportunity as a youth to take part in sport.

Brother of above. Married Mary Aynscombe Mossop in 1871, two sons.

BAKER, Alfred Joseph

England unofficial matches 1,2,3.

Born 10 February 1846 in Willesden, Middlesex; died 3 January 1900 at Willesden.

Brought up in Kilburn, school not known. He was involved in association football right from the start, selected in the Secretary's XIV in January 1864. Played for NNs Kilburn (along with several brothers) and for Wanderers from 1867. Represented Middlesex (1867-68), Kent (1868), captained South v North (1870); he appears to have stopped playing in 1871. An England selector for the second and third internationals, he served on the FA committee 1871-72. He won the AAA 100 yards in 1870. Having served an apprenticeship with Driver & Co of Whitehall, Baker took over his father's property business, Baker & Sons, and grew it into a highly profitable auction house, specialising in the sale of land for development; he was a surveyor to the Board of Trade. President of the Harlesden Conservative Association. He died on the platform at Willesden Junction while running to catch his train.

Son of Henry Baker, estate agent and surveyor, and Margaret Puddicombe, Married Ellen Marion Sayers in 1871, two sons, three daughters before her death in 1878; married Margaret Ellen Sayers, his dead wife's sister, and had another six sons.

BAKER, Thomas Southey

England unofficial match 4.
Born 29 June 1848 in Droxford, Hampshire; died 24 June 1902 in Dunedin, New Zealand.
Lancing (1861-67), football XII and cricket XI. Queen's College, Oxford (BA 1871), where he was a triple rowing blue, victorious in 1869 and on the losing side in 1870-71. Played football for Clapham Rovers. Was briefly a master at the Whitgift School before he emigrated in 1873 to New Zealand. He devoted his life to teaching at schools in Christchurch, Tasmania, Otago and finally Dunedin.
Son of Dr Thomas Baker and Sophia Jane Southey. Married Josephine Harriet Anne Dicken in 1878, four daughters, of whom Eleanor became famous as a pioneering surgeon.

BARKER, Robert
England internationalist.
Born 19 June 1847 in Wouldham, Kent; died 11 November 1915 in Watford, Hertfordshire.
Marlborough College (1858-62) where he played rugby but on leaving school took up association rules. Played mainly for Hertfordshire Rangers, but also for Wanderers. His only cap was in 1872. A civil engineer with the South Eastern & Chatham Railway, he lived in Rickmansworth, where his father was vicar, and later in London before retiring to Watford.
Son of Rev Alleyne Higgs Barker and Marianna Burminster. Did not marry.

BETTS, Morton Peto

England unofficial matches 3,4; England internationalist.
Born 30 August 1847 in Bloomsbury, London; died 19 April 1914 in Garavan, France.

106

Harrow (1862-65). From 1870 he played for West Kent and famously scoring the winning goal for Wanderers in the first FA Cup final of 1872, under the pseudonym AH Chequer, in honour of the Harrow Chequers club. He played in goal for England v Scotland in 1877, also represented Kent, London and the South v North (1870). On FA committee 1871-73 and 1881-90, becoming vice-president. Played cricket for Middlesex and Kent, and was honorary secretary of Essex. An enthusiastic promoter of baseball, he was secretary of the National Baseball League of Great Britain in the 1890s. He travelled to the USA in 1865 to launch his career as a civil engineer, and regularly worked overseas, in South America from 1873-76 and in Denmark at the end of the decade. He retired to the south coast of France for the last three years of his life.

Son of Edward Ladd Betts, a railway contractor who was bankrupted in 1867 along with his brother-in-law Sir Morton Peto, and Ann Peto. Married Jane Bouch in 1879, two daughters; after her death in 1892 he married Jane Morgan in 1901.

BONSOR, Alexander George
England unofficial match 5; England internationalist.

Born 7 October 1851 at Polesden Lacey, Great Bookham, Surrey; died 17 August 1907 in Brussels, Belgium.

Eton (1865-68). Played for Wanderers, winning the FA Cup in 1872 and 1873, then for Old Etonians in their cup finals of 1875 and 1876. Capped twice by England, in 1873 and 1875, and represented Surrey and London. He was a director of Combe & Co, the family brewing business, until 1893.

Son of Joseph Bonsor and Eliza Denne Orme. May have married first Marie Charlotte c1880, one daughter; second Jeanne Marie David in 1893, divorced 1896; third Claire Marie Silvie Kint in 1897; no further children.

BOWEN, Edward Ernest

England unofficial match 1.

107

Born 30 March 1836 in Glenmore Castle, County Wicklow, Ireland; died 8 April 1901 in Moux, France.

Educated at Lille, Southwark, Blackheath Proprietary School (1846-51), King's College, London (1852-54), and Trinity College, Cambridge (BA 1858). An occasional player for Wanderers from 1865, he won FA Cup winners' medals with them in 1872 and 1873. In cricket, he played one first class match for Hampshire in 1864. He was appointed a Classics master at Harrow School in 1859, and remained in post for the rest of his life.

Son of the Rev Christopher Bowen of County Mayo and Katherine Emily Steele. Did not marry.

BROCKBANK, John
England internationalist.
Born 22 August 1848 in Whitehaven, Cumberland; died 4 February 1896 in Fulham, London.

Shrewsbury School (1865-67), cricket and football elevens. Trinity College, Cambridge (BA 1873). Won one cap in 1872, was also a football blue (March & November 1874) and represented London v Sheffield four times. Played with Wanderers and Clapham Rovers. Cricket for the MCC and Cumberland. North of England at athletics in 1872 and won many prizes for sprinting and hurdling. An actor in Covent Garden under the name of John Benn or John Benn Brockbank.

Son of James Brockbank, solicitor, and Jane Nicholson. Married May Pimm in 1878, three daughters.

BUTLER, William Charles
England unofficial matches 1,3.
Born 17 January 1844 in Birkenhead, Cheshire; died 6 December 1914 in Carlisle, Cumberland.

Played football with Barnes from 1868-71, then for Civil Service for a year. He entered the Civil Service in April 1862, as a clerical assistant in the Probate Court, and in the mid-1870s he moved to Carlisle, where he ran the Probate Registry office until his retirement. Also served as a volunteer in the 36th Middlesex Rifle Volunteer Corps, becoming Lieutenant in 1872, and later in the Cumberland militia.

Son of Captain Charles George Butler RN and Emily Bayford. Married Emily Chadwick in 1877, three sons and three daughters.

CARTER, Thomas Nevile
England unofficial match 2.
Christened 16 September 1851 at Eton (no record of birth); killed by lightning 16 November 1879 in the Transvaal, South Africa.

Eton (1864-71), in the College, Mixed Wall and Field elevens, and Keeper of the Field. Editor of the *Eton College Chronicle* in 1871. Career not known.

Son of the Rev William Adolphus Carter, Fellow of Eton, and Gertrude Rogers. Did not marry.

CHAPPELL, Frederick

Scotland unofficial match 3; England internationalist.

Born 22 July 1849 in London; died 25 September 1907 in Berlin, Germany.

Marlborough Royal Free Grammar School. Brasenose College, Oxford (BA 1874). Won the FA Cup twice, with Oxford University in 1874 (losing finalist in 1873) and Wanderers in 1876, playing for the latter until 1880. Played for England v Scotland in 1872, and represented South v North (1870), Surrey v Middlesex (1872) and London v Sheffield three times. An athletics blue for Oxford in 1871. He was called to the bar in 1876, but disbarred at his own request in 1884 to become a solicitor, and ran Metzler & Co, a music company.

Son of Frederick Patey Chappell and Eleanor Maddison. He changed his name to Frederick Brunning Maddison on 5 February 1873. Married Katherine Mary Adela Tindal in 1883, one son, one daughter.
Image courtesy Rita Wellstead.

CHENERY, Charles John
England unofficial match 5; England internationalist.

Born 1 January 1850 at Lambourn, Berkshire; died 17 April 1928 at Mansfield, Victoria, Australia.

Marlborough Royal Free Grammar School (1862-68), cricket XI. He came to London on leaving school and played football for Wanderers and Crystal Palace. Selected for England in the first three full internationals, 1872-74, also played for South v North (1870). A member of London Athletic Club, competing in races 1868-71. Played for Surrey at cricket in 1872-73. He emigrated to Australia in 1878, and became a cattle station manager at Mansfield, Victoria.

Son of George Chenery, farmer, and Sophia Atkins. Married Priscilla Swan in 1890, three sons.

CLEGG, John Charles

England unofficial match 5; England internationalist.

Born 15 June 1850 in Sheffield; died 26 June 1937 in Sheffield.

Known as Charles, he was educated privately in Sheffield and Darlington. He played for Sheffield FC, The Wednesday and other local clubs; selected for Sheffield against London and Glasgow. Played for England in the first official international in 1872, his brother William in the return later that season. Referee of the 1882 and 1892 FA Cup finals, he joined the FA committee in 1886, was appointed chairman when Council was formed in 1890, and President in 1923, holding the position until his death. A prominent athlete in Sheffield from around 1867, he was reputed to have won over 100 prizes and according to his obituary, 'He never went into training, but kept himself in condition by ordinary exercise and a rigid adherence to temperance principles.' A solicitor, in 1872 he became a partner in his father's company, WJ Clegg & Sons. Official Receiver in Bankruptcy. He was knighted in 1927 for services to the Board of Trade. President of the British Temperance League.

Son of William Johnson Clegg and Mary Sykes. Married Mary Sayles in 1872, two sons and one daughter.

COCKERELL, John

England unofficial matches 2,3.

110

Born 22 November 1845 in Camberwell; died 27 January 1937 in Surbiton, Surrey.

Played football for Crystal Palace 1865-68, then for Brixton (club captain) and Barnes. Selected for Surrey and Kent in 1867, Surrey in 1868 (twice) and 1869. An all-round sportsman, he was a prominent athlete in London. Worked as a clerk for his uncle's company, George Cockerell & Co, coal merchants.

Son of John Brand Cockerell and Ellen Field. Married Jessie Green in 1872, at least four sons and two daughters. *Image courtesy Bill Kalkhoven.*

CONGREVE, Galfrid Francis
Scotland unofficial match 2.

Born 16 July 1849 at Danevale, Kirkcudbrightshire; died 10 February 1882 in Stormont Road, Clapham.

Brought up in Castle Douglas, southern Scotland. Although listed as an Old Rugbeian, he was educated at Keir House, a private school in Wimbledon, where he captained the football team. His appearances at association football were sporadic, although he did play for Civil Service in the 1874/75 FA Cup. Instead, he chose to play rugby football and did so with success as captain of Ravenscourt Park, a prominent London club; he came close to

being capped at rugby for England, playing in two international trial matches in 1874. A member of the London Athletic Club and the Amateur Athletic Club, he won the mile race in the prestigious Civil Service Sports, three times. He was a member of the MCC but did not play cricket at first class level. In the Civil Service, he worked in the Exchequer & Audit Office Examining Branch, then the Board of Trade, from 1870 until his early death, age 32.

Son of Richard Jones Congreve and Louisa Margaret Miller. Did not marry.

CRAKE, William Parry

England unofficial matches 1-4.

Born 11 February 1852 in Madras, India; died 1 December 1921 at Norfolk Crescent, Hyde Park, London.

Known as Parry. Harrow (1866-70) football XI, cricket XI.

Played for Harrow Chequers and Wanderers, winning the FA Cup in 1872. Represented Middlesex and South v North (1870). Played cricket for Harrow Wanderers. He went to India, following in his father's footsteps as a senior manager of Parry & Co, one of the biggest trading companies in Madras. While there he played cricket, tennis and racquets for the Madras Presidency. He returned to England in 1884, resumed cricket with the MCC and Free Foresters, and took up golf, shooting and fishing.

Eldest son of William Hamilton Crake and Jane Wood. Married Emily Noble Chase in 1881, two sons.

CRAWFORD, Fitzgerald Hamilton

Scotland unofficial matches 4,5.

Born 5 May 1854 in Edinburgh; died 7 October 1894 at 6 Hans Place, London.

Brought up in Edinburgh, moved to north London in 1864 and appears to have been educated privately. Played for Harrow Chequers. Elected a Fellow of the Royal Geographical Society in 1878, as was his father, and gave this as his occupation. Listed as a 'gentleman' in probate, he left an estate worth £2,818.

Son of General Robert Fitzgerald Crawford and Jane Dalrymple Anderson. Surname became Copland-Crawford in 1872. Did not marry.

CRAWFORD, Robert Erskine Wade

Scotland unofficial matches 1,2,4,5.

Born 5 September 1852 in Elizabeth Castle, Jersey; died 23 May 1894 in Sudbury Lodge, Middlesex.

Harrow (1866-71), cricket XI. Played cricket for the MCC in 1872-73. A Lieutenant with the 60th (King's Royal) Rifles, he served in the Afghan War in 1879-80, and the Sudan campaign 1883-84. Appointed to the Sierra Leone police in 1888, he was convicted the following year of killing a servant.

Brother of above. Surname became Copland-Crawford in 1872. Married Helen Elizabeth (Nellie) Steuart in 1882, divorced 1883, one daughter.

ELLIOT, Edward Hay Mackenzie

Scotland unofficial matches 4,5.
Born 30 November 1852 in Vizagapatam, India; died 5 December 1920 in London.
Windlesham and Harrow (1866-70). Played for Wanderers 1871-73, in FA Cup semi-final of 1872 against Queen's Park, but not the final; also for Harrow Chequers, and once for London v Sheffield (1872). 'A truly ponderous player but successful as a dribbler,' according to the 1873 *Football Annual*. In his military career he was Major in the South Lancashire Regiment (Prince of Wales Volunteers); Lieutenant 82nd Regiment 1874; Instructor of Musketry 1882; Captain 1884; transferred to 40th Regiment 1888; Major 1894;

ADC to the Earl of Glasgow, Governor and Commander in Chief of New Zealand, 1894; retired 1899. Had a magnificent moustache (see photo). The Elliots of Wolfelee were a historic Scottish borders family but he was born in India as his father, an official in the Indian Civil Service, was Senior Member of Council in the Madras Presidency (which contained Vizagapatam). Edward succeeded to the family estate after his two elder brothers died but sold Wolfelee, near Hawick, in 1912 and went to live in Springfield, Hereford.
Son of Sir Walter Elliot KCSI and Maria Dorothea Hunter Blair. Married Edith Margaret Crawford in 1905, no children.

FERGUSON, Harold Stuart
Scotland unofficial matches 4,5.
Born 10 February 1851 in Park Street, London; died 5 January 1921 in London.
Eton (1861-67) and Wimbledon (1867-69), where the football team generally played rugby rules. Came fifth in the entry exam to the Royal Military Academy, Woolwich, and duly obtained a commission in the Royal Artillery in 1872. Resigned in 1874 but remained on the reserve, and returned to service in 1914 as a captain in the London Rifle Brigade. He went to India where he worked for the

Maharajah of Travancore, and in time was appointed director of the Trivandrum Museum and Public Gardens. On retiring to London in 1904, he continued to devoted himself to natural history, and was elected to the council of the Zoological Society.
Son of Dr Robert Ferguson, professor of obstetrics, and Mary Macleod. Married Isabel Julia Maxwell in 1875, three sons.

FREETH, Evelyn
England unofficial match 1.
Born 25 May 1846 in London; died 16 September 1911 at Lymington, Hampshire.
Eton (1855-64). Played football for Civil Service and Old Etonians. Entered the Civil Service in 1864 as a clerk in the Legacy and Succession Duty Office, Somerset House, dealing with death duties. Moved to Dublin in 1884 as Deputy Controller, Legacy & Succession Duties, Ireland, and from 1900-02 was Registrar of Estate Duties for Ireland. Recalled to London as Registrar of the Estate Duty Office until 1908, when he was knighted. He retired to New Milton and his grave is in the churchyard there.
Son of Charles Freeth and Anna Elizabeth Turner. Married Florence Thompson Oakes in 1870, four sons and four daughters.

GARDNER, Robert

Scotland internationalist.
Born 31 May 1847 in Glasgow; died 28 February 1887 in South Queensferry.
Captain of Queen's Park and therefore captain of Scotland, he selected the team for the first international in 1872 and won four further caps, the last being the 7-2 victory over England in 1878, generally playing in goal. Having been a founding member of Queen's Park in 1867, he joined Clydesdale in 1874 after a disagreement, playing for them in that year's Scottish Cup final, and remained with that club until his retirement in 1880. Elected president of the Scottish FA in 1877-78. He worked as a grain salesman in Glasgow but lost his job and latterly was employed as a contractor's clerk on the Forth Bridge construction project; his wife was a cousin of William Arrol, the main contractor. Died of tuberculosis.

Son of Robert Gardner, grain miller's clerk, and Janet Cochran. Married Mary Arrol in 1873, three sons.

GLADSTONE, William Henry

Scotland unofficial matches 1,3.
Born 3 June 1840 in Hawarden Castle, Flintshire, Wales; died 4 July 1891 in London.
Eton (1852-59) and Christ Church, Oxford (BA 1862). At Eton, where he was a close friend of the Prince of Wales, he played the field game, and won the Fives competition, but rarely played sport after leaving school. Said to be shy and retiring, he had the advantage of strength and height, standing over six feet. He was MP for Whitby and a Junior Lord of the Treasury when he played for Scotland; he also represented Chester and East Worcestershire during his political career. His abiding passion was music: he wrote

religious anthems and organ voluntaries, publishing *A Selection of Hymns and Tunes* (1882). His last few years were blighted by brain disease and a series of strokes, and he died after an operation to remove a brain tumour. At the time of his death he was a JP and a Deputy Lieutenant for the county of Flint. Caricatured in *Vanity Fair* as 'His Father's Son' (*pictured*).
Eldest son of William Ewart Gladstone, Prime Minister, and Catherine Glynne. Married Gertrude Stuart, daughter of Lord Blantyre, in 1875, one son (killed in action in 1915) and two daughters.

GORDON, George Croughly

Scotland unofficial match 1.
Born 21 June 1850 in Kensington, London; died 20 August 1899 in Cue, Western Australia.

115

Clapham Grammar School. A player with CCC (Clapham), Civil Service and NNs (Kilburn), his main sport was rowing and he won a number of prizes, most notably the Grand Challenge Cup in 1876 with Thames RC. Entered the Civil Service in 1867 as a clerk, and in the late 1870s emigrated to New Zealand, then Australia. In the 1880s his engineering company constructed the Cape York Telegraph Line. Later a mining agent in Western Australia, where he died.

Son of Cosmo William Gordon and Ellen Hensley. Married Mary Agnes Wallace in 1889, one son.
Image courtesy Alistair Gordon.

GREENHALGH, Ernest Harwood
England internationalist.
Born 6 March 1849 in Mansfield, Nottinghamshire; died 11 July 1922 in Mansfield.
Known as Harwood, he was one of the pioneers of soccer in Nottingham, and spent his entire career with Notts Football Club (now Notts County) from 1867 to 1883, captaining them in the FA Cup semi-final in his last season. He later became secretary of Greenhalgh's FC in Mansfield, which had been founded by his father. He was proprietor of the Field Mill (which gave its name to the ground of Mansfield Town), a major cotton mill with around 400 staff.

Son of Herbert John Greenhalgh, lace manufacturer, and Emma Anne Leavers. Married Anne Wilson in 1874, but after she died married Kate Goddard in 1898.

HAMILTON, *see Baillie-Hamilton*

HOGG, Quintin

Scotland unofficial matches 2,3.
Born 14 February 1845 in London; died 17 January 1903 in London.
Eton (1858-63), Wall and Field XI, won Fives, in shooting team. Played for Wanderers 1866-1871, and for Old Etonians in the 1876 FA Cup final. Hogg made his fortune in the tea and sugar trade, as senior partner in Hogg, Curtis, Campbell and Co, and was chairman of North British and Mercantile Insurance. Best known as a philanthropist and educationist, he founded the Regent Street Polytechnic, which provided technical education to

thousands of young men and women. Founded Hanover United in 1875 as a football club for the Polytechnic, and played with them in the FA Cup as late as 1883. Inaugurated Quintin Rugby Club in 1885, and what is now the Quintin Boat Club by paying £800 for a club house. Published *The Story of Peter*, a collection of his lectures, in 1900. Son of Sir James Weir Hogg and Mary Swinton. Married Alice Anna Graham, daughter of William Graham MP, in 1871, three sons, two daughters.

HOOMAN, Thomas Charles

England unofficial matches 2,3,5.
Born 28 December 1850 in Kidderminster, Worcestershire; died 22 September 1938 in Hythe, Kent.
Charterhouse (1863-68), football XI, cricket XI. Played for Old Carthusians, North v South (1870) and won the FA Cup with

Wanderers in 1872. Was selected for England in the first two official internationals, but was ill or unavailable, and appears to have retired from football thereafter. A sporting all-rounder at athletics and rowing (as was his son Charles who won blues at cricket, golf and rackets). Started in business as a ship insurance broker, then went into cement manufacturing. Lived in Kent before retiring to Torquay and spent his final years in Hythe.
Third son of James Hooman of Highgate, carpet manufacturer, and Mary Ann Hemming. Married Louisa Holt in 1879, one son, one daughter.

INGLIS, John Frederic

Scotland unofficial match 3.
Born 16 July 1853 in Peshawar, India; died 27 February 1923 in Exmouth, Devon.
Charterhouse (1864-71) football XI, cricket XI. Described in the

1868 *Football Annual* as 'by far the smallest in the eleven, but by no means the worst player,' he appears to have given up football when he left school. Played cricket for Kent in 1883. A career soldier, he joined the 62nd Regiment of Foot in 1873, which became the Duke of Edinburgh's (Wiltshire) Regiment in 1881, and retired as Major in 1898.

Son of Lieut-Col Sir John Eardley Wilmot Inglis KCB and Julia Selina Thesiger. Married Janet Alice Thornhill in 1886, no children. His younger brother Rupert won three caps for England at rugby. *Image courtesy Charles Inglis.*

KENNEDY, Gilbert George
Scotland unofficial match 2.
Born 9 May 1844 in Bath, Somerset; died 2 January 1909 in Thanet, Kent.

Harrow (1858-63) football XI, and Trinity College, Cambridge (BA 1868). Played for Wanderers 1866-74, and was a member of the FA committee 1868-70. An athletics blue in 1867 (two mile race) and 1868 (three mile race), he also rowed bow in the First Trinity Eight. A barrister on the Midland circuit, he was Recorder of Grantham, a Metropolitan Police Magistrate at Greenwich & Woolwich from 1889-1907, and a JP, all of which gave him ample experience which he used to contribute to a number of legal books, such as *A Guide to the Coal Mines Regulation Act, 1887.*

Youngest son of John Kennedy, Secretary of Legation in the Diplomatic Service at St Petersburg, Naples and Washington, and Amelia Maria Briggs. His father died before his first birthday. Married Alice Lyon in 1874, four sons.

KENRICK, Jarvis
England unofficial match 4.
Born 13 November 1852 in Chichester, Sussex; died 29 January 1949 in East Blatchington, Sussex.

Lancing College (1861-69). With Clapham Rovers he scored the first ever goal in the FA Cup in 1871, then with Wanderers he won the FA Cup three times in 1876-78, scoring in the latter two. FA committee 1877-79. Played cricket for Surrey in 1876, and was captain of Redhill and Reigate Golf Club. Spent his working life as a solicitor, based in Bletchingley, Surrey. Retired to Wimbledon then the Sussex coast. The last survivor of the international pioneers, he is commemorated by a plaque in St Mary's Church, Bletchingley.

Only son (with six sisters) of Rev Jarvis Kenrick, curate of Horsham, and Etheldred Hodgson. Married Lilian Helen Jaffray in 1884, nine daughters.

KER, William

Scotland internationalist.

Born 21 March 1852 in Edinburgh; died 3 December 1925 in Washington DC, USA.

Played for and captained Granville and was also captain of Queen's Park. Capped by Scotland in the first two internationals, he was honorary treasurer of the Scottish FA on its foundation. Emigrated to Canada in 1873, initially as a banker, before working in the fledgling telephone industry in England and Pennsylvania. He moved to Washington state as a land manager, and finally Washington DC as a real estate dealer, retiring around 1915.

Son of Dr John Kerr, lecturer in mathematics, and Marian Balfour. Married Lizzie (Lily) Florence Bell in 1876, three sons, one daughter. He changed the spelling of his surname from Kerr to Ker at an early age. *Image courtesy Graham Johnson.*

KINNAIRD, Arthur Fitzgerald

Scotland unofficial matches 1,2,3; Scotland internationalist.

Born 16 February 1847 in Hyde Park Gardens, London; died 30 January 1923 in St James's Square, London.

Eton (1861-65) and Trinity College, Cambridge (BA 1868). Played mostly for Old Etonians and Wanderers, with whom he won five FA Cups and appeared in nine finals between 1872 and 1883, a record. Capped once for Scotland in 1873. An FA committee member from 1868, treasurer 1878-90, then President until his death, a total of 55 years. A banker, he was a partner with Ransom Bouverie & Co from 1870, and following a merger became a director of Barclays Bank. A prominent philanthropist and evangelical Christian, he worked in ragged schools with Quintin Hogg from his schooldays, and became a

119

passionate supporter of many good causes; president of the YWCA and YMCA.

Son of Arthur Kinnaird MP and Mary Jane Hoare. Married Mary Alma Victoria Agnew in 1875, six sons, two daughters. Succeeded his father as 11th Lord Kinnaird in 1887.

KIRKE-SMITH, *see Smith*

KIRKPATRICK, James
Scotland unofficial matches 1-4.
Born 22 March 1841 in Hamburgh, Canada; died 10 November 1899 in Forest Hill, Kent.

Appears to have been educated privately. Had an unusually lengthy football career with Civil Service and Wanderers from 1866, and won the FA Cup with Wanderers in 1878. Represented Surrey and Kent (1867). FA Committee 1868-72. Played cricket for Civil Service, West Kent and once for Gentlemen of the South. Entered the Civil Service in 1861 as a temporary clerk, and rose to become private secretary to the First Lord of the Admiralty. In 1880, he succeeded his brother as 8th Baronet of Closeburn.

Second son of Charles Sharpe Kirkpatrick, Baronet, and Helen Stuart Kirk. Married Mary Steward Fearnley in 1872, four sons, two daughters.

LECKIE, Robert

Scotland internationalist.
Born 19 October 1846 in Killearn, Stirlingshire; died 25 November 1886 in Olifants Bosch, South Africa.

A right-sided forward, he played in the first international, and won the Scottish Cup with Queen's Park in 1874, retiring the following year. Went to South Africa, and died in the Mankazana valley. His family owned Spittal Farm in Killearn, where his brother Alexander continued as a prize-winning Clydesdale Horse breeder; the buildings are still there, developed into a family home.

Son of John Leckie and Margaret McGregor. Did not marry.

LINDSAY, William

Scotland unofficial matches 1-5; England internationalist.
Born 3 August 1847 at Benares, India; died 15 February 1923 in Rochester, Kent.
Winchester (1858-65), cricket XI. The only player to represent Scotland in all five of the unofficial internationals, he was later capped for England in 1877 despite having no birth link; his family came from Dundee. His early football was with Civil Service and Rochester, then he seems to have stopped playing for a few years in the early 1870s; however, he joined Wanderers in 1875 in time to feature in three successive FA Cup winning sides, 1876-78. He played 33 matches of cricket for Surrey 1876-82 and won the hurdle race at the Civil Service Sports three years in a row, 1869-71. In 1867 he started work as a junior clerk in the store department of the India Office and from 1877 to 1881 was private secretary to the Under-Secretary of State, then in 1882 became senior clerk. He was private secretary to Lord George Hamilton, Hon Edward Stanhope, the Marquis of Lansdowne and Viscount Enfield before he retired in 1900.
Son of Major William Lindsay, Bengal Native Infantry, and Lillias Don. Married Emily Agnes Edwardes in 1871, one daughter, one son.

LUBBOCK, Edgar

England unofficial matches 1-5.
Born 22 February 1847 in Westminster, London; died 9 September 1907 in Hans Court, Chelsea, London.
Eton (1857-66), mixed wall and field elevens, cricket captain, won Eton Fives three times. London University (LLB 1874). Captained West Kent, then won the FA Cup with Wanderers in 1872, and played for Old Etonians in three finals, losing in 1875 and 1876 but winning in 1879. Represented Kent v Surrey (1868 and 1869), South v North (1870), London v Sheffield (1875). Played cricket once for Kent in 1871, and toured North America with the MCC the following year. An excellent lawn tennis player, he competed at Wimbledon and won the South of England championships. Master of Blankney Hunt. He used his law degree to good effect, becoming a director of Whitbread Brewery from 1875, rising to managing director. A director of the Bank of England,

he was appointed deputy governor a few months before his death. Profiled in *Vanity Fair* in 1906, he was said to have 'a stout heart, a sound business head, and a humorous twinkle in his eye'. He was buried in Caythorpe, Lincolnshire, where he lived his final years.

Eighth and youngest son of Sir John Lubbock and Harriet Hotham, and the fifth to go to Eton where he was known accordingly as 'Quintus'. Married Amy Myddelton Peacock in 1886, three daughters.

MACKINNON, William Muir

Scotland internationalist.

Born 18 January 1852 in Gorbals, Glasgow; died 24 May 1942 in Cambuslang, Lanarkshire.

Won nine Scotland caps in the 1870s, scoring five goals against England, and also played in the first three Scottish Cup finals, winning them all and scoring a goal in 1874 and 1875. Although his career was spent with Queen's Park, he also made a guest appearance for Rangers in their very first match in 1872. Worked as a clerk for P&W MacLellan, a major engineering concern in Glasgow. When Mackinnon died aged 90, the last of the original internationals, his obituary in the *Glasgow Herald* almost completely ignored his place in football history, and was headed 'Veteran Glasgow Musician', highlighting his role with city musical groups including the Glasgow Male Voice Choir.

Son of James McKinnon [sic] and Margaret McGill. Married Margaret Purcell Conner in 1883, three daughters, two sons.

MADDISON, *see Chappell*

MALCOLM, John Wingfield

Scotland unofficial match 1.

Born 16 April 1833 in Stratford Place, London; died 6 March 1902 at Hyères, France.

Known as Wingfield. Eton (c1845-1851) and Christ Church, Oxford (BA 1856). An imposing physical presence, he was 6 feet 5 inches tall, said to tower 'head and shoulders above even average Scotchmen,' and he added to the impression by sporting a luxuriant black beard. At the time of the match he was Conservative MP for Boston (1860-74) and later for Argyllshire (1886-92). He was made Lord Malcolm of Poltalloch in 1896; he was also a CB, JP, and Deputy Lieutenant of Argyllshire.

Son of John Malcolm, a renowned art collector who left him £80,000, and Isabella Harriet Wingfield. Married Alice Frederica Irby in 1861; after her death in 1896, married Marie Jane Lilian Lister in 1897; both marriages were childless.

MAYNARD, William John
England internationalist.
Born 18 March 1853 in Camberwell, London; died 2 September 1921 in Sunderland.

Played mainly for 1st Surrey Rifles, a Camberwell side, and occasionally for Wanderers. In the 1872 international, Maynard was the youngest player in the England line-up at 19 years, 157 days; he won a second cap in 1876. Represented Surrey in 1877. He became a clerk in the courts (like his father) and in 1903 was appointed district probate registrar in Durham, retaining the post until his death. Son of William Maynard and Elizabeth Connolly Stent. Married Annie Smith in 1883, five children; son Alfred played rugby for England but was killed in the First World War.

MITCHELL, Hugh

Scotland unofficial matches 4,5.
Born 3 December 1849 in Cavendish Road West, London; died 16 August 1937 in Brakpan, South Africa.

Harrow (1864-67), shooting XI. Royal Military Academy, entered Royal Engineers in January 1870. Played for Royal Engineers in 1872 FA Cup Final. Rose to the rank of Captain 1882, with postings in Bermuda and Gibraltar, then left the RE to study law and became a barrister

123

in 1884 (but remained an honorary Lieutenant at the Building Works Department, Woolwich Arsenal). In 1896 he set up a legal practice in Gibraltar and Tangier. Mitchell was a great classical scholar, had a bookcase full of prizes from his time at Harrow, and liked to enliven conversation with puns in Greek and Latin. However, after the death of his wife he became withdrawn and a granddaughter remembered him as 'a patriarchal and terrifying figure'.

Son of Lieut Colonel Hugh Mitchell, Madras Native Infantry, and Jessie McCaskill. Married Mary Catherine Edwards (Katie) Cresswell in 1878 (sister of RE team mate Edmund Cresswell); she died when giving birth to their seventh child. Their son Sir Philip Mitchell was Governor of Uganda, Fiji and Kenya.

MORICE, Charles John
England internationalist.
Born 27 May 1850 in Paddington, London; died 17 June 1932 in Hampstead, London.
Harrow (1865-67). Captain of Barnes, also played for Harrow Chequers and Wanderers. The international cap was his only honour. FA committee 1873-78. He was a stockbroker in London.

Eldest son of Charles Walter Morice, stockbroker, and Sophia Levien. Married first to Rebecca Gould (née Garnett), one daughter; secondly Clementina Francis (née Turvey), one son. His younger brother William played for Barnes, Clapham Rovers and Brentwood; he was a cousin of England international Percy de Paravicini; grandfather of actors Edward and James Fox; great-grandfather of actress Emilia Fox.

MORTEN, Alexander
Scotland unofficial match 1; England internationalist.
Born 1831/2 in Paddington, London; died 24 February 1900 in Earls Court, London.
School not known. He played from at least 1863 with NNs of Kilburn, 1866-74 with Crystal Palace (as captain and in the inaugural season of the FA Cup) and regularly with Wanderers from 1865. Represented London v Sheffield (1866 and 1874), South v North (1870). He was a veteran by the time he captained England against Scotland in March 1873 aged 41 and appears to have retired from playing in 1874. FA committee member 1874-75. Played cricket for Kensington Park and Crystal Palace. A broker in the London Stock Exchange. Member of the Royal Colonial Institute.

His parents are unknown. Married Flora Hedger in 1855, two sons, four daughters.

MUIR MACKENZIE, Kenneth Augustus

Scotland unofficial match 1.
Born 29 June 1845 at Delvine, Perthshire; died 22 May 1930 in London.
Charterhouse (1857-1864), cricket and football captain. Balliol College, Oxford (BA 1868). Played for Old Carthusians. FA committee 1868-70. A barrister and civil servant, entered Lincoln's Inn 1869, called to the bar 1873, QC 1886, Principal Secretary to the Lord Chancellor 1880-1915, Clerk of the Crown 1885-1915. CB 1893, KCB 1898, GCB 1911 and in 1915 made Baron Muir-Mackenzie. Elected Warden of Winchester College 1904, the first non-Wykehamist in 500 years. Buried in Westminster Abbey.
Son of John William Pitt Muir Mackenzie, 2nd Baronet of

Delvine, and Sophia Matilda Johnstone. Married Amelia (Amy) Margaret Graham, sister of Quintin Hogg's wife Alice, in 1874, one son, three daughters.

MUIR MACKENZIE, Montague Johnstone

Scotland unofficial match 5.
Born 29 September 1847 at Delvine, Perthshire; died 18 April 1919 in London.
Charterhouse (1860-1866), football captain, cricket XI; won 100 yards (*see picture*). Brasenose College, Oxford (BA 1870), Fellow of Hertford College 1874-88. He joined Wanderers on leaving school, and also played for Old Carthusians. Won Brasenose mile race in 1868. Called to the bar 1873, Recorder of Deal 1892, Recorder

of Sandwich 1894, counsel to the Board of Trade, JP. Author of *Notes on the Temple Organ* and other legal works.
Brother of above. Married Sarah Napier Bruce, daughter of Lord Aberdare, in 1888, one daughter.

NASH, Alexander Andrew Ellis

England unofficial match 1.
Born 30 August 1849 in Edmonton, Middlesex; died 18 July 1906 in Gilfach, Glamorgan. Brentwood Grammar School (1862-67), football and cricket elevens. Played for Wanderers and CCC, then joined Clapham Rovers late in 1869, becoming club captain. Played for England in March 1870, South v North (1870), on FA committee 1872-74. Won putting the shot at club sports in April 1870. His football career was partially echoed by his cousin AJ (Andrew John) Nash, who was educated at Repton and also played for Clapham Rovers; both took part

in the first FA Cup competition. A merchant in London, he became a member of the Merchant Taylors' Company in 1870, but little about his later life is known except that he was living off a trust worth £20,000 at the time of his death on holiday, which a coroner's inquest concluded was due to chloral hydrate poisoning; no charges were brought.
Son of William Nash, of Edmonton and Ilford, and Caroline Fairbanks. Married Harriette Jane Routledge in 1896, no children. His sisters married into sporting families, and at least three nephews were university blues.

NEPEAN, Charles Edward Burroughs

Scotland unofficial matches 2-5.
Born 5 February 1851 in Westminster, London; died 26 March 1903 in Hollingbourne, Kent.

126

Charterhouse (1861-69), football captain for three years; cricket captain for two years. University College, Oxford (BA 1873). Played for Wanderers and Gitanos while still at school, and won an FA Cup winners' medal in 1874 with Oxford University. In cricket, he won a blue in 1873, played for Middlesex 1873-74, for Gentlemen v Players in 1873, and for Gentlemen of Kent v Philadelphia in 1884. He was ordained in 1874 and became vicar of Lenham in Kent in 1876, where he remained for the rest of his life.

Son of Evan Nepean, Canon of Westminster and Chaplain in Ordinary to Queen Victoria, and Anne Fust. Did not marry. Gt gt gt uncle of actor Hugh Grant.

OTTAWAY, Cuthbert John

England internationalist.

Born 19 July 1850 in Dover, Kent; died 2 April 1878 in Sloane Square, London.

Eton (1863-69), cricket eleven, winner of Public Schools Rackets Cup. Brasenose College, Oxford (BA 1874). One of the finest sportsmen of his day, he captained Oxford University to FA Cup success in 1874, was a beaten finalist in 1873, and was again on the losing side for Old Etonians in 1875. He also played for both Marlow and Crystal Palace in the 1871-72 FA Cup. FA committee 1872-74. A four-times cricket blue for Oxford, ultimately as team captain, he was also a blue in athletics, rackets and real tennis, a total of five sports which remains a record to this day. Called to the bar in 1876, he hardly had time to practise before his untimely death from pneumonia.

Only child of Dr James Cuthbert Ottaway, surgeon and former mayor of Dover, and Jane Bridge. Married Marion Elizabeth Stinson in 1877, who was pregnant with their daughter Lilian when he died.

PATON, Walter Boldero
England unofficial match 2.
Born 19 April 1853 in Westminster, London; died 11 February 1937 in Kensington, London.

127

Harrow (1866-72), captain of football, won 100 yards. University College, Oxford (BA 1876). Played in the 1873 FA Cup Final for Oxford University and subsequently for Harrow Chequers and Old Harrovians. He was publications editor at the Emigrants' Information Office.

Son of George Paton, barrister, and Laura Blagrove. Married Adeline Henrietta Loftus, maid of honour to Queen Victoria, in 1892, two sons.

PRESTON, Henry Jacob

England unofficial match 2.
Born 15 September 1851 at Beeston Hall, Beeston St Lawrence, Norfolk; died 9 January 1897 at Northrepps, Cromer, Norfolk.
Eton (1865-71) wall and field elevens, rowing eight. University College, Oxford (BA 1876). Served from 1876 in the Prince of Wales's Own Norfolk Artillery.

Succeeded his father as baronet in 1891.
Son of Sir Jacob Henry Preston and Amelia Prescott. Married Mary Hope Clutterbuck in 1885, three sons and two daughters.

PRIMROSE, Gilbert Edward
Scotland unofficial match 3.
Born 27 February 1848 at Barnbougle, Midlothian; died 16 February 1935 in Worthing, Sussex.
Trinity College, Glenalmond (1858-65), cricket XI. Went to Australia in 1873 and founded the Helidon Spa Water Company. A captain in the Queensland Scottish Rifles and the Queensland Defence Force, JP. Retired to England in 1909.
Son of Hon Bouverie Francis Primrose, son of the Earl of Rosebery, and Hon Frederica Sophia Anson. Married Jessie Katherine Costelloe in 1893, no children.

PRIMROSE, Henry William
Scotland unofficial match 2.
Born 22 August 1846 in Barnbougle, Midlothian; died 17 June 1923 in Kensington, London.
Trinity College, Glenalmond (1855-64), captain of school and captain of cricket. Balliol College, Oxford (BA 1868). Entered the Treasury in 1869 as a clerk and in the course of his career was

private secretary to the Viceroy of India 1880-84 and to the Prime Minister (Gladstone) 1886; secretary to the Office of Works and Public Buildings; chairman of the Board of Customs 1895-99, and chairman of the Board of Inland Revenue 1899-1907. CB 1895, knighted 1899. He died in tragic circumstances: suffering from depression and chronic insomnia, he went to Kensington Gardens, near his home, and shot himself with his Webley revolver. Brother of above. Married Helen Mary McMicking in 1888, one son.

RAVENSHAW, Edward Vincent
Scotland unofficial match 5.
Born 30 July 1854 in Mortlake, Surrey; died 23 May 1880 near Jalnacherra, India.
Bromsgrove School (1865-66) and Charterhouse (1866-1872) cricket XI and football XI. Played football for Old Carthusians briefly after leaving school. He worked as a clerk in the Old Bank, Malvern, then was offered a job as a tea planter in India. However, after a couple of years he drowned in the Katakhal river in Assam.
Son of George Chandler Ravenshaw and Eliza Willock; did not marry. His uncle Thomas founded Ravenshaw College (now University) in Orissa.

RENNY-TAILYOUR, Henry Waugh

Scotland unofficial match 4; Scotland internationalist.
Born 9 October 1849 in Mussoorie, northern India; died 15 June 1920 in Montrose, Angus.
Cheltenham College (1859-1867) cricket XI. Royal Military Academy, Woolwich (1868-70). Played for Royal Engineers in the FA Cup finals of 1872, 1874 and 1875. Played for Scotland at rugby and association football, the only man to have done so. In his Royal Engineers career he was made Major (1888), Lieut Colonel (1895) and Brevet Colonel (1899). After retiring, he became managing director of Arthur Guinness & Son.
Son of Colonel Thomas Renny-Tailyour, Bengal Engineers, and Isabella Eliza Atkinson. Married Emily Rose Wingfield-Stratford (sister of England international CV Wingfield-Stratford) in 1875, four sons and six daughters.

RHIND, Alexander

Scotland internationalist.

Born 20 September 1849 in Aberdeen; died 13 December 1923 in Inverness.

Only spent a couple of years in Glasgow with Queen's Park, winning one Scotland cap, and left the club in November 1873 to go north for business reasons. A commercial traveller for a wholesale drapery business, he worked in Aberdeen until about 1892, thereafter in Inverness.

Son of Alexander Rhind and Margaret Gray. Married Isabella Anderson McRuer in 1877, six sons, four daughters.

SMITH, Arnold Kirke

Scotland unofficial matches 3,4; England internationalist.

Born 23 April 1850 in Ecclesfield, Yorkshire; died 8 October 1927 in Boxworth, Cambridgeshire.

Cheltenham College (1863-1867), football XX. University College, Oxford (BA 1873). Having played for Scotland twice in unofficial internationals, thanks to a Scottish grandfather, he was then capped for England in the first match against Scotland in 1872 (his jersey sold at Christie's in 1998 for £21,000). A football blue for Oxford, he captained the University in the 1873 FA Cup final. Also kept close contact with football in Sheffield, representing the city against Derbyshire and London in 1873, and played for Sheffield FC in 1873-74. Represented North of England at athletics (1872) and played cricket (with Charles Nepean) for University College. Ordained in 1875, he had various charges before serving as rector of Boxworth from 1889 until his death. Keen on beekeeping.

Son of William Smith, a brewer whose family was instrumental in introducing football to Sheffield, and Mary Anne McKenzie. Married Emma Frances Lindsell in 1877, three sons. He seems to have adopted the surname Kirke-Smith at Oxford without ever formally changing it.

SMITH, Giulio Cowley Tyler

England unofficial match 1.

Born 2 May 1849 in Piccadilly, London; died 22 July 1909 at Links, Seaford, Sussex.

Westminster School (1863-1868), football XI. Played for Middlesex (1867) while at school, then for Old Westminsters, Crusaders, Flying Dutchmen and

NNs. A talented athlete, he won the Westminster mile race and 100 yards. Member of London Athletic Club. Tea and coffee merchant with John Cassell and Co, London. Joined Middlesex Rifle Volunteer Corps in 1868, resigned his commission in 1872 (on the same day as his brother Ernest).

Son of Dr William Tyler Smith, obstetric surgeon, and Tryphena Yearsley. Married Florence Isabel Gadesden in 1878, no children. Regularly named as JC Smith, apparently based on a phonetic rendering of his first name as Julio; later in life he adapted his surname to Tyler-Smith. *Image courtesy Carol de Poy.*

SMITH, James

Scotland internationalist.
Born summer 1844 in Aberdeen; died 20 September 1876 in Urquhart, Moray.
A founding member of Queen's Park in 1867, he served as club treasurer for two years. Went to

London in 1871, following in the footsteps of his brother, and played for South Norwood, including regular FA Cup ties, until early 1876. Made one international appearance in 1872. An artist's traveller (a salesman for artistic supplies), he died at his parents' home of a stroke.
Son of Robert Smith, gardener to the Earl of Fife, and Barbara Abercrombie. Did not marry.

SMITH, Robert

Scotland unofficial matches 2,3,4; Scotland internationalist.
Born 1 May 1848 in Aberdeen; died 3 June 1914 in Chicago, Illinois, USA.
A founding member of Queen's Park in 1867, he joined South Norwood in 1869 while retaining his QP membership. Played in three unofficial internationals as well as winning two full caps. FA committee 1871-73. Educated at Fordyce Academy, he went to Glasgow in 1864, then to London in 1869 and emigrated to Wyoming in 1873, where he

founded the *Sweetwater Gazette* newspaper. In 1903 he was appointed to the Indian Service in Oklahoma, and after two years set up his own business dealing in oil concessions.

Brother of James, above. Married Georgina Kidd in 1879, one son, one daughter.

STEPHENSON, Charles William
England unofficial matches 3,4,5.
Born 27 February 1853 in London; died 22 April 1924 in London.

Westminster School (1864-71), football XI, cricket XI. Played for Wanderers while still at school, and in their first two FA Cup ties. Also for South v North (1870) and London against Sheffield (1871-72), but appears to have given up playing by the time he was 20. FA committee 1871-73; he was present at the meeting in July 1871 that decided on the foundation of the FA Cup. A quantity surveyor, based in Parliament Street, London. Member of the Queen's Westminster Rifles.

Son of Charles Stephenson and Mary Anne Lansdown. Married Charlotte Harriet Underwood in 1877, two daughters.

STEWART, Henry Holmes
Scotland unofficial match 5.
Born 8 November 1847 in Cairnsmore House, Newton Stewart, Kirkcudbrightshire; died 20 March 1937 at Strathella, Dinas Powys, Wales.

Loretto (1859), Repton (1861-67) cricket XI. Trinity College, Cambridge (BA 1871). Won FA Cup with Wanderers in 1873. Played cricket for MCC, I Zingari and Gentlemen of Yorkshire. Ordained 1872, he was curate of St John, Holborn 1872-74, vicar of East Witton, Yorkshire 1874-78, rector of Brington, Northants 1878-98, rector of Porthkerry with Barry, Wales, 1898-1914, vicar of St Lythan, Cardiff 1914-25, rector of Michaelston-le-Pit, Glamorgan 1925-34.

Ninth son of James Stewart and Elizabeth Macleod. Married Lady Beatrice Cecilia Diana Carnegie, daughter of the Earl of Southesk, in 1874, three sons, two daughters.

TAYLOR, Joseph

Scotland internationalist.

132

Born 16 December 1850 in Dunoon, Argyll; died 4 October 1888 in Mount Florida, Glasgow. His early grounding in sports came in Dunoon's annual Cowal Gathering, where he won nine athletic contests in 1869 and 1870. Coming to Glasgow, he joined Queen's Park and played in the first three Scottish Cup finals, winning them all, and was capped by Scotland in all of the first six internationals. He had given up playing by the time he was elected QP club president for 1878-79. A mercantile clerk in a drapery warehouse, he died at home of tuberculosis and pleurisy; Queen's Park played a benefit match for his widow and children.

Son of John Taylor, hotel keeper, and Ann McLean. Married Agnes Cumming Miller in 1879, four sons.

THOMPSON, Albert Childers

England unofficial matches 4,5.

Born 13 July 1848 in Kirby Hall, Ouseburn, Yorkshire; died 20 March 1894 in Marylebone, London.

Eton (1860-67), Oppidan wall XI, shooting team. Trinity College, Cambridge University (BA 1871). Having kept up his football at Cambridge, where he played for the Eton Club, he won the FA Cup with Wanderers in 1872 and also played for Old Etonians in the 1875 and 1876 finals, but not in either replay. As well as two unofficial internationals for England he represented London, Surrey and Middlesex. [NB His playing career is sometimes confused with that of Arthur Thompson (Harrow), another prominent player with Wanderers.] Called to the bar in 1872, he worked on the North-Eastern circuit and at the Parliamentary Bar. He was made a QC in 1892 but his health broke down through over-work and he went to Colorado to recover. On the boat home he caught a chill and died of acute bronchitis three days after returning.

Son of Sir Harry Stephen Thompson, and Elizabeth Ann Croft. The family surname changed to Meysey-Thompson in February 1874 when Sir Harry was created 1st Baronet. Married Mabel Louisa Lascelles in 1882, one son.

THOMPSON, Charles Maude

Scotland unofficial match 5.
Born 5 December 1849 in Kirby Hall, Ouseburn, Yorkshire; died 11 September 1881 in Peoa, Utah, USA.
Eton (1860-68), Trinity College, Cambridge (BA 1872). Played football at university then joined Wanderers, winning the FA Cup with them in 1873. He was also a runner-up with Old Etonians in 1876 (first game only). At Cambridge he was an athletics blue in 1872, throwing the hammer. Ordained in 1873, he was curate at Whitby then at St Pancras, and rector of Claydon, Buckinghamshire from 1876-79. In declining health, he travelled to Utah to try and recover in the hot dry climate, but died there.
Brother of AC Thompson, above. Changed surname to Meysey-Thompson in 1874. Married Emily Mary Walker in 1874, one son, one daughter.

THOMSON, James John

Scotland internationalist.
Born 25 December 1851 at Millfield, Annan; died 21 July 1915 in Highgate, London.
Missed Queen's Park's 1872 FA Cup semi-final through injury but captained the side to victory in the Scottish Cup in 1874 and played in the first three internationals. His cup medal and international cap are in the Scottish Football Museum. Gave up the game in 1874 for a job in the meat trade with Eastman and Co, initially in Liverpool and then moved to London, becoming chairman and managing director. Left £46,000 in his will.
Son of James Thomson and Nicholas Bell. Married Sarah Thomson Dunbar in 1880, two sons, one daughter.

THORNTON, Alfred Horace
England unofficial match 1.
Born 27 January 1853 in Rawalpindi, India; died 31

134

March 1906 at Bank House, Windsor.

Harrow (1867-69), football XI. Played for Wanderers and Harrow Chequers. He spent his early years in the Punjab, where his father was Commissioner for Rawalpindi. Entered the banking business on leaving school and became manager of the Old Bank and Brewery at Windsor, an unusual combination of businesses which was not split up until several years after his death. He was a Berkshire JP.

Son of Edward Thornton CB, Indian Civil Service, and Louisa Chicheliana Plowden. Did not marry.

VIDAL, Robert Walpole Sealy

England unofficial matches 1-5; England internationalist.

Born 3 September 1853 at Cornborough House, Abbotsham, Devon; died 5 November 1914 at Abbotsham.

Known as Walpole. Westminster (1867-72), captain of cricket and football. Christ Church, Oxford

(BA 1876). Selected for all five unofficial internationals, he also played in the first three FA Cup finals, with Wanderers (1872) and Oxford University (1873, 1874). His only cap for England was against Scotland in 1873. Represented South v North (1870). Uniquely, he won blues for both association and rugby football at Oxford. FA Committee 1872-73 and 1874-75. Ordained in 1877, he was vice-principal of Ely College then vicar of Abbotsham from 1881 until his death.

Third son of Edward Urch Vidal and Emma Harriet Eyre. Married Gertrude Molesworth in 1885, one son and three daughters. Changed surname to Sealy in 1892. *Image © David Rice.*

WALKER, Robert Sandilands Frowd

England unofficial matches 2,3,4.

Born 13 May 1850 in Chester Castle; died 16 May 1917 at Scotia Lodge, Knockholt, Kent.

Brentwood Grammar School, football eleven. Royal Military College, Sandhurst. Joined CCC (Clapham) in 1868, then played for Clapham Rovers. A career soldier, he joined the 28th North Gloucestershire Regiment and in 1896 formed the Malay States Guides, Indian Army. Came out of retirement to act as commandant of the Alexandra Palace Prisoner of War Camp.

Son of John Walker, ordnance storekeeper, and Camilla Walker. Married Beatrice Bolton (née Ireland) in 1896, no children. Adopted the surname Frowd-Walker.

WEIR, James Biggar

Scotland internationalist.
Born 23 November 1851 in Gorbals, Glasgow; died 23 April 1889 in Warrina, South Australia.
Played regularly for Queen's Park until 1880, winning four caps for Scotland, scoring twice in his final appearance. He also won the Scottish Cup three times, in 1874, 1875 and 1880. A joiner to trade, he emigrated to Australia in 1881, and died of typhoid fever and congestion at a railway construction post.

Son of William Weir, joiner and builder, and Agnes Biggar. Marriage details unknown.

WELCH, Reginald Courtenay

England internationalist.
Born 17 October 1851 in Paddington, London; died 4 June 1939 in Farnham, Surrey.
Known as Courtenay (which he altered to 'de Courtenay'). Harrow (1864-71), cricket and football elevens. Won the FA Cup with Wanderers in 1872 and 1873, but usually played for Old Harrovians and Harrow Chequers. Won two caps for England, 1872 and 1874. FA committee 1873-76 and 1879-81. A tutor of Law at the Lower Temple, later an Army tutor, he

became Principal of the Army College in Farnham. Edited the *Harrow Register*. Chairman of the Throat Hospital in Golden Square, London.

Son of John Welch, a special pleader, and Henrietta Anne Fowell Sprye. Married Adeline Charlotte Compton in 1888, one son (Walter, killed in action).

WESTON, Percy

England unofficial matches 4,5.
Born 27 March 1852 in Hackney, London; died 30 June 1905 in London.

School not known. Played for Barnes FC from 1868 until at least 1875, mainly as goalkeeper but also up front, and he scored for Barnes in one of the first FA Cup ties, with his brothers Edward and Vincent in the same team. Represented London v Sheffield 1871-72. FA committee 1872-73. The five Weston brothers came from a prominent

Putney rowing family, whose small stature made them ideal coxes, and Percy won several prizes with London Rowing Club from 1865-71 (sometimes in the same boat as FA pioneers RG Graham, RW Willis and EC Morley). In 1871 he entered the Amateur Boxing Championship, but lost in the first round and was described as 'a very poor opponent'. A stockbroker, he lived at Greenfields, East Sheen.

Son of John Weston, merchant and financial agent, and Augusta Ellen Wood. Married Blanche Katharine Williams in 1873, four sons and five daughters; their son Spencer was a Brigadier General.
Image courtesy David Weston.

WOLLASTON, Charles Henry Reynolds
England unofficial match 5; England internationalist.
Born 31 July 1849 at Felpham Vicarage, Sussex; died 22 June 1926 in Victoria, London.

Lancing College (1862-68), football captain, cricket XI. Trinity College, Oxford (BA 1871). Won the FA Cup five times with Wanderers, the first man to do so (1872, 1873, 1876, 1877, 1878), and played four times for England v Scotland between 1874 and 1880; referee in 1879. Represented Middlesex v Surrey (1875). FA Committee 1879-86. Qualified as a solicitor

137

in 1875 but never practised, and joined the Union Bank of London in 1878, later being appointed a director. A keen mountaineer, he made regular climbing trips to the Swiss Alps and was secretary of the Alpine Club.

Son of Rev Charles Buchanan Wollaston and Eleanor Reynolds. Did not marry.

initially as a clerk at an iron merchant, and by 1881 was employing two men. At his death, from tuberculosis, he was described as a lime quarry shareholder.

Son of William Wotherspoon, baker, and Mary Hamilton. Married Mary Galbraith in 1876, five daughters.

WOTHERSPOON, David

Scotland internationalist.

Born 9 April 1849 in Hamilton, Lanarkshire; died 28 February 1906 in Pollokshields, Glasgow.

On the Queen's Park committee from 1869-74, as secretary 1869-72. Played for Scotland in the first two internationals. Joined Clydesdale with Robert Gardner in 1874 and played for them in the Scottish Cup final that year. His brothers Thomas and John also played for Queen's Park. He worked in the metal trade,

Chapter 10

RUGBY PLAYER BIOGRAPHIES

The first rugby football internationalists
Scotland v England, 27 March 1871

SCOTLAND

ARTHUR, John William
Born 25 April 1848 in Glasgow;
died 15 March 1921 while on
holiday in Saint Jean de Luz,
France.
Glasgow Academy and Glasgow
Academicals. Mainstay of the
Accies for many years, his
international cap survives with
the club. A businessman in
Glasgow, he was a director of the
city's Chamber of Commerce. He
was a member of the 4th
Lanarkshire Rifle Volunteers in
his youth, and heavily involved
in army recruitment in the early
days of the First World War.

BROWN, William Davie
Born 29 May 1852 in Glasgow;
died 24 March 1876 near
Blantyre, Lanarkshire.
Glasgow Academy and Glasgow
Academicals. He played in the
first five internationals then

retired from rugby after
captaining Scotland in March
1875. A year later he was killed
by a train.

BUCHANAN, Angus
Born 15 January 1847 in
Inveraray, Argyllshire; died 21
February 1927 in Aberfeldy,
Perthshire.
Royal High School (Edinburgh)
and FPs. Scored the first try in
international football. A banker,
he was resident agent for the
National Bank of Scotland in
Edinburgh, Kirkwall and
Paisley.

CHALMERS, Thomas
Born 19 March 1850 in Glasgow;
died 25 May 1926 in Glasgow.
Glasgow Academy and Glasgow
Academicals. Played in the first
six rugby internationals. He also
played a trial for the first
association football international
in 1872 and was an outstanding

139

cricketer, batting for Scotland against Yorkshire and the MCC, and for West of Scotland against the Australians. A stockbroker.

CLUNIES-ROSS, Alfred
Born 1851/2 in New Selma, Cocos Islands; died 27 February 1903 in Cocos Islands.
Madras College. Enrolled at St Andrews University (1868-69) then Edinburgh University to continue his medical studies but did not graduate. While in Edinburgh he played for Wanderers but was described as a St Andrews University player in the international. Worked as a doctor in London until the mid-1880s, then in Borneo 1888-1901 when illness forced him to return home. The Clunies-Ross family, originally from Shetland, were *de facto* rulers of the Cocos Islands and Alfred's father John was hailed as King of the Cocos. His mother, S'pia Dupong, was Malay, so Clunies-Ross qualifies as the first non-white international player.

COLVILLE, Andrew Galbraith
Born 17 December 1846 in Campbeltown; died 19 April 1881 in Bournemouth, Dorset.
Merchiston. Moved to London after leaving school and was playing for Blackheath at the time of the international.

Worked in Luanda (in what is now Angola) during the 1870s.

CROSS, William
Born 10 September 1850 in Ayr; died 16 October 1890 in Bournemouth, Dorset.
Merchiston, Glasgow Academy, and for both schools' former pupil clubs. Scored a conversion and a try in the international. His brother Malcolm was later a Scotland international and SRU president.

DREW, Daniel
Born 13 October 1850 in Glasgow; died 2 February 1914 in Habergham Eaves, Lancashire.
Glasgow Academy and Glasgow Academicals, then played for Manchester after moving to Lancashire in the early 1870s. He ran a calico printing factory in Burnley employing 500 people.

FINLAY, James Fairbairn
Born 8 April 1852 in Edinburgh; died 25 January 1930 in Guildford, Surrey.
Edinburgh Academy (dux of the school, captain of football and cricket) and Academicals. Edinburgh University. Entered Indian Civil Service in 1875, and was Secretary to the Government of India Finance and Commerce Department, but retired in 1908 through ill health.

FORSYTH, William
Born 23 March 1850 in Edinburgh, died 12 March 1935 in London.
Edinburgh Institution and Edinburgh University. Qualified as a doctor and worked for the Indian Medical Service 1876-1910, based in Calcutta. Elected a Fellow of the Royal College of Surgeons of Edinburgh, and of the Society of Antiquaries of Scotland, in 1911. Lived in Wales then Berkshire before his death.

IRVINE, Robert William
Born 19 April 1853 in Blair Atholl, Perthshire; died 18 April 1897 in Pitlochry, Perthshire.
Madras College, Edinburgh Academy and Academicals. The most enduring of the first internationals, 'Bulldog' played against England every year from 1871-80, and three times against Ireland, 13 caps in all, eight as captain. Edinburgh University. A much-loved doctor in Pitlochry, a memorial to him in the town's cemetery was raised by public subscription.

LYALL, William John Campbell
Born 27 January 1848 in Edinburgh; died 22 April 1931 in Kansas, USA.
Edinburgh Academy and Academicals. Emigrated in 1871 to USA and settled in Athol, Kansas, where he was a farmer.

McFARLANE, John Lisle Hall

Born 19 June 1851 in Montego Bay, Jamaica, died 17 March 1874 in Edinburgh.
Edinburgh Institution, Abbey Park (St Andrews) and Edinburgh University, where he qualified as a doctor in 1873. Also a talented athlete and cricketer, he died after a rugby injury led to him contracting a fever. A memorial (*pictured*) was raised by public subscription in Edinburgh.

MARSHALL, Thomas Roger
Born 26 June 1849 in Belford, Northumberland; died 27 June 1913 in Kingfield, Cumberland.
Edinburgh Academy and Academicals, then Edinburgh University. Qualified as a lawyer then worked for a time as a coffee planter in India. Played cricket for Scotland and the MCC. His brother William played in the second rugby international.

MEIN, James
Born 1 July 1852 in Jedburgh; died 2 March 1918 in Kelso.
Edinburgh Academy and Academicals. Edinburgh University. A farmer in the Scottish borders, on inheriting an uncle's farm in 1890 he changed his name to James Andrew Whitelock Mein. Went bankrupt in 1913 and lost both properties.

MONCREIFF, Francis Jeffrey
Born 27 August 1849 in Edinburgh; died 30 May 1900 in Edinburgh.
Edinburgh Academy and Academicals. Captain of the first Scotland team. A Chartered Accountant, he was a founder of the Scottish Investment Trust and a director of the Bank of Scotland. His father James was Lord Advocate of Scotland.

MUNRO, Robert
Born 26 April 1853 at Mudale House, Strathnaver, Sutherland; died 5 February 1919 at Barclay Manse, Old Kilpatrick, Dunbartonshire.
Strathy School and St Andrews University. After graduating in 1873 he studied for the ministry at New College, Edinburgh and was appointed minister of the Barclay Free Church at Old Kilpatrick in 1878. An antiquary of note, awarded an honorary degree by St Andrews in 1916.

RITCHIE, George
Born 16 April 1848 in Edinburgh; died 31 January 1896 in Kelso.
Edinburgh Academy, Merchiston and Merchistonians. A brewer, he succeeded his father as owner of Bell's Brewery, Pleasance, Edinburgh, where Edinburgh University sports centre now stands.

ROBERTSON, Alexander Hamilton
Born 1 October 1848 in Ayr; died 12 May 1913 in London.
King William's College (Isle of Man), Edinburgh Academy and West of Scotland, which he captained for several seasons. An influential figure who was a signatory to the challenge letter to the English in December 1870. He was a stockbroker in Glasgow, then moved to London.

THOMSON, John Shaw
Born 9 August 1845 in Glasgow; died 22 May 1925 in London.
Glasgow Academy and Glasgow Academicals. He worked for his father George's company, Laird & Thomson, shawl and dress manufacturers in Glasgow; then became a merchant in London. Left £25,000 in his will.

* * *

142

ENGLAND

BENTLEY, John Edmund
Born 17 January 1847 in Calver, Derbyshire; died 12 December 1913 in West Hampstead.
Merchant Taylors School and Gipsies, also a member of London Athletic Club. Worked in the Civil Service as a clerk in the Supreme Court of Judicature. His son Edmund invented Clerihews, an irreverent form of verse.

BIRKETT, Reginald Halsey
Born 28 March 1849 in London; died 30 June 1898 in Wimbledon.
Lancing College and Clapham Rovers. His club played both codes, and Birkett made the most of the opportunities, winning four caps for England at rugby, then honours at association football including a cap for England in 1879 and two FA Cup finals in 1879 and 1880, the latter being victorious. A skin and hide broker in London, he leaped to his death from a window while delirious with diphtheria.

BURNS, Benjamin Henry
Born 28 May 1848 in Perth, Scotland; died 3 June 1932 in Christchurch, New Zealand.
Edinburgh Academy. The son of a bank manager, he moved to London and played for Blackheath while beginning a career in international banking which took him to India, Japan, China, Australia and New Zealand.

CLAYTON, John Henry
Born 24 August 1848 in Liverpool; died 21 March 1924 in London.
Rugby School and Liverpool. A cotton broker in Liverpool, he did much to popularise rugby football in Lancashire.

CROMPTON, Charles Arthur
Born 21 October 1848 in Cork, Ireland; died 6 July 1875 in Cherat, Punjab.
Congleton School and Royal Military Academy, Woolwich. He joined the Royal Engineers in 1869 but played rugby for Blackheath. Was on service with the Bengal Sappers and Miners when he died of an abscess of the liver. His grave at Peshawar describes him as 'Strong, brave and straight-forward, faithful, honourable & true'.

DAVENPORT, Alfred
Born 5 May 1849 in Oxford; died 2 April 1932 in Abingdon, Oxfordshire.
Rugby School, Balliol College, Oxford and Ravenscourt Park. He was first captain of the Oxford University rugby club. A solicitor in London.

DUGDALE, John Marshall
Born 15 October 1851 in Eccles, Lancashire; died 30 October 1918 in Llanfyllin, Montgomeryshire.
Rugby School and Ravenscourt Park. Graduated in law from Brasenose College, Oxford, worked as a barrister on the northern circuit, in Cheshire then Montgomeryshire.

GIBSON, Arthur Sumner
Born 14 July 1844 in Fawley, Hampshire; died 23 January 1927 in East Hampstead, Berkshire.
Marlborough College, Trinity College, Oxford. After graduating he became a civil engineer in Lancashire and played rugby for Manchester.

GREEN, Joseph Fletcher
Born 28 April 1846 in West Ham, London; died 28 August 1923 in Leeds, Yorkshire.
Rugby School and West Kent. Brother-in-law of Frederic Stokes, he was injured in the international and apparently never played again. Played cricket for Gentlemen of the South and MCC. A ship owner.

GUILLEMARD, Arthur George
Born 18 December 1845 in Eltham, Kent; died 7 August 1909 in Eltham.
Rugby School and West Kent. A committee member of the RFU from its foundation until his death, he served as its president from 1878-82 and was renowned for his knowledge of the game. He also played association football for Forest FC. A solicitor in London and Kent.

HAMERSLEY, Alfred St George
Born 3 October 1848 in Great Hasely, Oxfordshire; died 25 February 1929 in Bournemouth.
Marlborough College and Marlborough Nomads. Captained England in 1874 for the last of his four caps. After being called to the bar he went to New Zealand where he is credited with starting rugby in Canterbury. Returning to England, he was elected MP for Mid-Oxfordshire 1910-18, and served in the First World War by recruiting and training men for heavy artillery batteries.

LUSCOMBE, John

Born 25 May 1848 in Lewisham, Kent; died 3 April 1937 in Crawley, Sussex.

School not known, played for Gipsies. His younger brother Francis also played for England. Spent his early adult life travelling the world in the Mercantile Marine, on ships owned by his father. A marine insurance underwriter, he was knighted in 1902 during the first of five spells as chairman of Lloyds.

LYON, Arthur
Born 4 August 1851 in Litherland, Lancashire; died 4 December 1905 in Christchurch, New Zealand.
Rugby School and Liverpool. He was a merchant in Liverpool before he emigrated in 1883. He spent three years in Minnesota, USA, on the way to settling in New Zealand where he took up farming. He was Master of Hounds with Christchurch Hunt Club.

MacLAREN, William
Born 12 January 1844 in Chorlton-upon-Medlock, Lancs; died 10 June 1916 in Witham, Essex.
School not known, he was elected captain of Manchester in 1868. A linen and home furnishings merchant in Salford. Also an athlete with Manchester AC, he came from a sporting family and his cousin James was president of the RFU.

OSBORNE, Richard Robinson
Born 20 May 1848 in Middleham, Yorkshire; died 4 November 1926 in Rochdale, Lancashire.
St John's College Hurstpierpoint. Played rugby for Rochdale and Manchester. Became a solicitor in Rochdale in 1873 and remained in the town for the rest of his working life. Played cricket for Rochdale. His brother was the jockey John Osborne.

SHERRARD, Charles William
Born 25 December 1849 in London; died 11 December 1938 in Beckenham, Kent.
Rugby School, Royal Military Academy and Blackheath. A career soldier, he joined the Royal Engineers in 1870 (on the same day as Scotland's HW Renny-Tailyour) and rose to the rank of Colonel before retiring in 1902. Served in the South African war of 1879. Last survivor of the first rugby international.

STOKES, Frederic
Born 12 July 1850 in Greenwich, Kent; died 7 January 1929 in Basingstoke, Berkshire.
Rugby School and Blackheath. Captain of England in the first three internationals, he played a key role in organising the contests. Was elected as the RFU's youngest ever president in 1874. One of six brothers to play

for Blackheath, one of whom, Lennard, was also capped by England and was RFU president. Played cricket for Kent and for Gentlemen v Players. A solicitor in London.

TOBIN, Frank
Born 23 September 1849 in Liverpool; died 6 February 1927 in Wavertree, Liverpool.
Rugby School and Liverpool. His father was Lord Mayor of Liverpool. Went to South America in 1872 as a merchant, living in Peru for 12 years, before returning to Liverpool where he was a partner in the stockbroking firm of Hornby, Tobin and Ockleston. Was made a CBE in 1920 for his work tending the wounded during the War.

TURNER, Dawson Palgrave
Born 15 December 1846 in Calcutta, India; died 25 February 1909 in Tunbridge Wells, Kent.
Radley College, Rugby School and Richmond. Played in the first five internationals against Scotland, and against Ireland in 1875. He joined the 47th (Lancashire) Regiment of Foot in 1865 but then trained as an obstetrician and practised in London.

TURNER, Henry John Cecil
Born 23 January 1850 in Hailsham, Sussex; died 27

September 1887 in Plympton St Mary, Devon.
Lancing College and Manchester. After working in Manchester as a bank clerk, he went to Calcutta, where he was a founding member of the India Tea Association in 1880, and wrote a treatise on tea before returning home. Lived at Velwell House, Buckfastleigh, Devon.

Timeline

1867

26 February   FA annual meeting ponders the future, Robert Graham elected honorary secretary

Summer   Robert Graham writes to every known football club in UK to promote association rules

9 July   Formation of Queen's Park FC, first Scottish club to play to association rules

2 November   Middlesex 0, Surrey and Kent 0 at Battersea Park, first county match

1868

25 January   Surrey 0, Kent 0 at Brompton

26 February   FA annual meeting, committee doubles in size to 12

14 November   Middlesex 1, Surrey 0 at Barnes

November   The *Football Annual* published for the first time, edited by Charles Alcock

1869

26 February   FA annual meeting, committee of 12 retained

27 February   Surrey 0, Kent 2 at Barnes

9 October   Wanderers 0, West Kent 2, first football match at Kennington Oval, London

1870

22 January   Letter published in *The Field*, advising of planned international between English and Scotch

19 February   Hard frost forces a postponement of international

23 February   FA annual meeting, Charles Alcock elected honorary secretary

5 March   **England 1, Scotland 1** at Kennington Oval, first unofficial international

19 November   **England 1, Scotland 0**, second unofficial international

6 December   Letter of challenge from Scottish rugby captains

16 December   Liverpool v Glasgow Academicals, first cross-border rugby football match

17 December   South 1, North 0, at the Oval

1871

26 January	Formation of Rugby Football Union in London
25 February	**England 1, Scotland 1**, third unofficial international
27 March	**Scotland defeat England** at Raeburn Place, Edinburgh, first rugby international
11 November	First FA Cup competition gets under way
18 November	**England 2, Scotland 1**, fourth unofficial international
2 December	Sheffield 3, London 1, first inter-city match

1872

27 January	London 1, Sheffield 0, inter-city match
5 February	**England defeat Scotland** at the Oval, second rugby international
24 February	**England 1, Scotland 0**, fifth unofficial international
2 March	Sheffield 2, London 1, inter-city match, one half each according to different rules
4 March	Wanderers 0, Queen's Park 0, FA Cup semi-final, first cross-border association football match
16 March	Wanderers win first FA Cup, defeating Royal Engineers 1-0 in the final
2 November	Sheffield 3, London 1, inter-city match
30 November	**Scotland 0, England 0** at Hamilton Crescent, Glasgow, first official football international

1873

3 March	Formation of the Scottish Rugby Union
3 March	**Scotland draw with England** at Hamilton Crescent, Glasgow, third rugby international
8 March	**England 4, Scotland 2** at the Oval, second football international
15 March	Formation of the Scottish Football Association.

Bibliography

CW Alcock, *Football: our Winter Game* (Field, 1874)

CW Alcock, *Football, the Association Game* (George Bell, 1890)

CW Alcock (ed), *The Football Annual*, 1868-1883

John Blythe-Smart, *The Wow Factor*, second edition (Blythe-Smart Publications, 2005)

John Blythe-Smart, *The Founders of Soccer* (Blythe-Smart Publications, 2008)

DD Bone, *Fifty Years' Reminiscences of Scottish Cricket* (Aird and Coghill, 1898)

The Book of Football (Amalgamated Press, 1906)

Keith Booth, *The Father of Modern Sport* (Parrs Wood Press, 2002)

Richard E Brock, *The Copland Crawfords of Wembley* (the author, 1989)

JAH Catton, *The Real Football* (Sands & Co, 1900)

WE Bowen, *Edward Bowen, A Memoir* (Longmans Green & Co, 1902)

JAH Catton, *Wickets and Goals* (Chapman and Hall, 1926)

Rob Cavallini, *The Wanderers FC, five times FA Cup winners* (Dog n Duck Publications, 2005)

Graham Curry, *Football: a study in diffusion* (University of Leicester thesis, 2001)

Lord Desborough (arr), *Fifty Years of Sport at Oxford, Cambridge and the Great Public Schools*, 3 vols (Walter Southwood & Co, 1916-1922)

Vic Duke and Liz Crolley, *Football Nationality and the State* (Longman, 1996)

Edinburgh Academical Football Club Centenary History (the club, 1958)

Morley Farror and Douglas Lamming, *A Century of English International Football 1872-1972* (Robert Hale & Co, 1972)

Alfred Gibson and William Pickford, *Association Football & The Men Who Made It*, 4 vols (Caxton, 1906)

Geoffrey Green, *The History of the Football Association* (Naldrett Press, 1953)

Geoffrey Green, *The History of the FA Cup* (Naldrett Press, 1949)

Glasgow Academical Club, *Centenary Volume 1866-1966* (Blackie, 1966)

Adrian Harvey, *Football: the first hundred years* (Routledge, 2005)

Luther B Hill, *A History of the State of Oklahoma* (Lewis Publishing Company, 1909)

Ethel M Hogg, *Quintin Hogg, a biography* (Constable, 1904)

R Ironside and AMC Thorburn, *Scotland v England 1871* (Scottish Rugby Union, 1971)

NL Jackson, *Association Football* (George Newnes Ltd, second edition, 1900)

Douglas Lamming, *A Scottish Soccer Internationalists' Who's Who, 1872-1986* (Hutton Press, 1987)

RR Lewis, *The History of Brentwood School* (the school, 1981)

Alfred Lubbock, *Memories of Eton and Etonians* (John Murray, 1899)

JA Mangan, *Athleticism in the Victorian and Edwardian Public School* (Cambridge University Press, 1981)

Maurice Marples, *A History of Football* (Secker and Warburg, 1954)

Charles JB Marriott & CW Alcock, *Football* (George Routledge, second edition, 1903)

Rev F Marshall, *Football, the Rugby Union Game* (Cassell & Co, 1892)

K McL Marshall and others, *Football Records of Rugby School 1823-1929* (George Over (Rugby) Ltd, 1930)

Tony Mason, *Association Football and English Society 1863-1915* (Harvester Press, 1980)

Andy Mitchell, *Arthur Kinnaird: First Lord of Football* (the author, 2011)

Philip Norman, *Scores and Annals of the West Kent Cricket Club* (Oxford University Press, 1897)

John J Pawson, *The Field Game* (Spottiswoode, Ballantyne & Co, 1935)

RJ Phillips, *The Story of Scottish Rugby* (TN Foulis, 1925)

William Pickford, *A Few Recollections of Sport* (Bournemouth Guardian, 1938)

DJC Pringle, *Lancing College to French Farm* (typescript biography of TS Baker held in Canterbury Museum, New Zealand, n.d.)

Progressive Men of the State of Wyoming (AW Bowen & Co, 1903)

Richard Robinson, *History of Queen's Park Football Club 1867-1917* (Hay Nisbet & Co, 1920)

Routledge's Football (George Routledge, 1867)

Richard Sanders, *Beastly Fury, the strange birth of British football* (Bantam Press, 2009)

Montague *Shearman, Athletics and Football* (Badminton Library, 1887)

Michael Southwick, *England's First Football Captain: a Biography of Cuthbert Ottaway* (Soccerdata, 2009)

RJ Spiller (ed), *The Early Years 1863-1878* (Association of Football Statisticians, 1983)

'Old International' [Alexander Steel], *25 Years Football* (John Menzies, 1890)

CD Stuart, *West of Scotland Football Club 1865-1965* (the author, 1965)

John Sugden and Alan Tomlinson, *Hosts and Champions* (Arena, 1994)

Keith Warsop, *The Early FA Cup Finals and the Southern Amateurs* (Soccer Data, 2004)

Frederick Wood, *Beeton's Football* (Frederick Warne & Co, 1866)

Percy M Young, *A History of British Football* (Stanley Paul, 1968)

Percy M Young, *Football in Sheffield* (Stanley Paul, 1962)

School, college and university registers

JM Anderson (ed), *The Matriculation Roll of the University of St Andrews 1747-1897* (William Blackwood and Sons, 1905)

AL Beasley (ed), *Merchiston Castle School Register 1833-1950* (Pillans and Wilson, 1951)

The Edinburgh Academy Register 1824-1914 (T&A Constable, 1914)

Old Etonian Association (comp), *Eton School Register, Part III 1862-1868* (Spottiswoode & Co, 1906)

J Foster (ed), *Alumni Oxonienses 1715-1886*, 4 vols (Parker, 1891-2)

The Glenalmond Register 1847-1954 (T&A Constable, 1955)

B Marsh and FA Crisp, *Alumni Carthusiana 1614-1872* (privately published, 1913)

A Register of St Nicholas College, Lancing 1848-1900 (privately published, 1900)

GF Russell Barker and Alan H Stenning, *The Record of Old Westminsters*, (Chiswick Press, 1928)

HEC Stapylton, *Eton School Lists 1853-1892* (R Ingalton Drake, 1900)

J Venn and JA Venn (eds), *Alumni Cantabrigenses*, 10 vols (Cambridge University Press 1922-54)

R de Courtenay Welch, *Register of Harrow School 1801-1893* (Harrow, 1894)

JRS Young (ed), *Edinburgh Institution 1832-1932* (George Waterson & Co, 1933)

Selected articles in magazines and periodicals

CW Alcock, Association Football (*English Illustrated Magazine* 88, January 1891, p282-288)

Anon., Football (*The London Review*, 23 January 1864, p84-85)

Michael Bentley, Gladstone's Heir (*English Historical Review*, Vol. 107, No. 425 (Oct. 1992), p 901-924)

Graham Curry, The Trinity Connection: An Analysis of the Role of Members of Cambridge University in the Development of Football in the Mid-Nineteenth Century (*Sport in History*, 22:2, p46-73, 2002)
CB Fry, Teams that have won the Football Association Cup (*Strand Magazine*, 23:136, April 1902, p455)
RG Graham, The Early History of the Football Association (*Badminton Magazine*, January 1899, p75-87)
Harold Macfarlane, Football of Yesterday and To-day, A Comparison (*Monthly Review* 25, October 1906, p129-138)

Index

Alcock, CW 14-33, 38, 43, 50-1, 55, 69, 91-2, 103, 147
Almond, HH 30, 35
Amateur Athletic Club 14, 18, 95, 111
Arthur, JW 30, 35, 139

Bailey, WH 27, 103
Baillie-Hamilton, CR 19, 97, 104
Baillie-Hamilton, WA 19, 27, 31, 97, 104
Baker, AJ 16, 18, 21-3, 25, 33, 105
Baker, TS 38, 40, 78, 106
Barker, R 33, 51, 54-5, 106
Battersea Park, London 7, 9, 14, 147
Bell, Alexander Graham 64, 67
Betts, MP 26, 28, 32-3, 38, 40-1, 50-1, 106
Bonsor, AG 43, 87, 107
Bowen, EE 17, 22, 76, 107
Bramall Lane, Sheffield 41, 50
Brentwood Grammar School 12, 17, 75
Brockbank, J 51, 55, 108
Brunning Maddison, *see* Chappell
Burns, BH 31, 34-5
Burrup, W 15
Butler, WC 20, 22, 32-3, 108

Cambridge University 38, 51, 76, 89, 90-1, 94
Carter, TN 26, 28, 32, 72, 101, 108
Chalmers, T 35, 48-9, 139
Chappell, F 3, 20, 32-3, 41, 50, 55, 57, 77, 94-5, 109
Charterhouse School 11, 13, 18-20, 26-8, 42, 72-3, 89

Chenery, CJ 41-3, 50, 55, 77, 94, 109
Civil Service FC 15, 19, 26-7, 79
Clapham Grammar School 12, 70
Clapham Rovers FC 12, 20, 26, 38, 41, 45, 51, 75
Clegg, JC 2, 41, 43, 48, 54-5, 92, 110
Cockerell, J 7, 26, 28, 32, 87-8, 110
Congreve, GF 27-8, 111
Crake, WP 17, 22, 26, 28, 33, 38, 40-1, 111
Crawford, FH 39-40, 43, 86-7, 112
Crawford, REW 16, 19, 21-3, 26, 28, 32, 39-44, 81-6, 112
Cross, W 34-5, 48-9

Edinburgh Academicals 29-30, 34
Elliot, EHM 39-40, 43, 113
Eton College 7, 10-11, 17-18, 26, 38, 72

Ferguson, HS 39-40, 43, 73-4, 113
Ferguson, RRN 19-20
Football Association 2, 7-8, 13-16, 20, 22, 25-6, 31, 42, 47, 50, 61
Freeth, E 17, 22, 114
Fulton, JN 42

Gardner, R 45, 50, 53-5, 114
Gladstone, WH 18, 22, 26, 31, 33, 42, 115
Glasgow Academicals 29-31, 35, 48
Gordon, GC 20, 22, 70, 115
Grace, WG 45, 88, 91
Graham, RG 13, 17, 137
Greenhalgh, EH 50, 55, 116

Hall Blyth, D 30, 34

153

Made in the USA
Charleston, SC
15 May 2012